# Living a Milk & Honey Life

*Tammy*
*Live the milk*
*& honey life!*
*Love,*
*Sharon Elliott*

# Living a Milk & Honey Life

### Letting Go of What's Holding You Back

Sharon Norris Elliott

BEACON HILL PRESS

OF KANSAS CITY

Copyright 2006
By Sharon Norris Elliott and Beacon Hill Press of Kansas City

ISBN 083-412-2480

Printed in the United States of America

Cover Design: Chad Cherry

### Library of Congress Cataloging-in-Publication Data

Elliott, Sharon Norris, 1957-
  Living a milk-and-honey life : letting go of what's holding you back / Sharon Norris Elliott.
    p. cm.
  Includes bibliographical references.
  ISBN 0-8341-2248-0 (pbk.)
 1. Christian women—Religious life. I. Title.

  BV4527.E445  2006
  248.8'43—dc22

                                                    2006000137

10  9  8  7  6  5  4  3  2  1

This book is dedicated
to my friends
ShaRon Cole and Debbie Price:
We talked and laughed about
the "Egypts" we had encountered,
and the leeks and onions we had consumed.
Now we are experiencing
three different paths.

ShaRon, the strength you need for your path
inspires me;
Debbie, the struggle you face on your path
humbles me;
may this book and our friendship
urge us all toward
more milk and honey than ever.

# Acknowledgements

My sincere and special thanks to the following:

God, my heavenly Father; Jesus Christ, my Lord and Savior; and the Holy Spirit, my source of power. This book is full of Your truth. Thanks for the material!

My wonderful husband, James D. Elliott, my knight and my strength. I love you. Thanks so much for believing in me and understanding the late hours at the computer to get this project completed.

My younger sons, Matthew and Mark, and my older kids, Lori and Jerod. Thanks for believing in me and being such incredible people. I can write and think clearly because you bring such joy to my life.

My students at South Bay Lutheran High School. All of you are incredible. You actually listen to what I have to say every day and keep me in touch with reality.

My sister-friends: Saundra, my "real" big sis; Cheryl and Meloni, you know which one is my favorite; Jean, my official fan-club president; Terri, super Auntie; Cissi, Tammy, Mary, and Diana. You ladies are my core. Every woman needs sister-friends like you!

Great Christian writers' conferences, especially Mount Hermon, Sandy Cove, and Glorieta. Your conference ministries are the reason for this book and all my writing successes. It's an honor being on staff.

My critique group. I know better than to submit anything anywhere before you ladies see it, tear it apart, and make me get it right. Special thanks to Jane Rumph on your line-by-line read-throughs and edit suggestions. I used almost all of them.

And Beacon Hill's own Perry ladies. Thanks for believing in the message of this book and for encouraging me every step of the way.

# Contents

# ▲ One
# Realization
### Where Am I and What Do My Taste Buds Like?

If you're like most of the women I talk to and hear about, you probably have something going on in your life right now—something that's occupying your thoughts and prayers. Maybe you're preoccupied with where you are right now in life and the direction you want your life to go. Maybe you're spending a lot of time thinking about what you like about your life and what you would like to change. What is dominating your thoughts and emotions? What are you dealing with? What is your issue? Is it a relationship? A parent or child issue? An education issue? Is there something going on at work, at church, with your weight, your finances, your friendships, your spirituality?

We are all dealing with something. Either we're in the midst of a problem or coming out of one. And if you're riding on easy street right now, just keep on living; a challenge is bound to be on its way. Life is not easy. And have you noticed that being a Christian hasn't made every challenge go away?

Indeed, life's journey is interesting and, unfortunately, it does not come with a warranty for a smooth ride. To the contrary, Jesus says, "Remember the words I spoke to you: 'No servant is greater than his master.' If they persecuted me, they will persecute you also" (John 15:20). The apostle Paul put it this way, "We are hard pressed on every side, but not crushed; perplexed, but not in despair; persecuted, but not abandoned; struck down, but not destroyed. We always carry around in our body the death of Jesus, so that the life of Jesus may also be revealed in our body" (2 Cor. 4:8-10).

OK, OK, I know. You're probably thinking, "I don't need somebody to tell me how bad things are. I'm reading this book in hopes that it will lift me up and help me live above my issues." Hang on. That's exactly what I want to do, but we're going to be realistic. I just want to encourage you that you don't have to pretend like everything's OK or that you're doing everything perfectly. Since life's journey can be a hard road, we're going to do some hard preparation. You're up to it. Let me start by telling you a little story.

When I was a child, my family took on the challenge of traveling cross-country by car almost every summer. My parents were from Maryland, and since they had moved to California, visiting relatives was a great reason to get to the East Coast every year. My father made us kids the navigators. We had to figure out where we were and where we wanted to go and then plot our course. Thanks to the map and those two fixed points—where we were and where we wanted to go—we always knew our location.

Now that I'm grown up, I still use maps. These days I either print them from my computer or use the navigational system in the car. I type in my address as the starting point and then type in the address of my destination. I press "enter" and up pops the directions and a detailed map or the voice of the satellite lady to tell me exactly where to go.

Although technology has advanced, the basic principle of travel has remained the same. In order to end up where I want to go, I must have a clear idea of where I am.

This book is going to take you on a journey to help you clearly identify exactly where you are and launch you toward the place God would have you go. The good news is you're not going alone. You will travel alongside the Israelites. The bad news is that you will not have the benefit of hindsight. Although they took this journey long before you did, you are going to travel with them as if this were the maiden voyage. It's more exciting this way. You'll experience the journey from bondage to deliverance firsthand and, hopefully, you'll experience the same thing for yourself.

However, you cannot move to where you want to go until you come to a full realization of where you are. Let's start by rating your satisfaction with your life as it is at the present moment. Using a scale of 1 to 10, with 10 meaning you're completely satisfied and 1 meaning you're totally dissatisfied, rate the issues of your life to get a realistic picture of your present location.

Are you spending most weekends satisfied, perhaps fulfilling some personal goals or with interesting people at interesting places? If the answer is yes, then your dating or friendship satisfaction level is high, perhaps a 10. Or are you staring at the phone, wishing it would ring with an invitation and feeling distraught when it doesn't? Rate that a 1. Is your marriage still like the honeymoon? Take a 10. Do you wish he was on the moon? Make it a 1. Is it exciting to go to work every day? That's a 10. Were you just thinking about quitting tomorrow? That's a 1. You get the idea.

Once you have rated the areas of your life on the chart (you can add other areas if you like), answer the final questions to round out this first picture of what you realize about yourself. What caused you to be in the place you are right now and were you prepared for it?

How satisfied are you with—
your dating or marriage relationship? ____
your relationship with your children? ____
your relationship with your parents? ____
your relationship with your friends? ____

your relationship with your coworkers? ____
your relationship with your boss? ____
your relationship with your subordinates? ____
your level of education? ____
your job or career? ____
your financial picture? ____
your residence? ____
the way you handle your emotions? ____
the way you look? ____
your health? ____
your service to others? ____
your life overall? ____

Check all of the following that apply to you:

I realize my life situation is a result of:
___ Choices I have made
___ Pure chance
___ Someone else's choices


Check one of the following:
My current situation (and/or issues) is what I expected:
___ Yes
___ No


I'm not going to analyze your answers. That exercise was just to get you thinking.

My friends and I were talking one day about the Israelites, and it dawned on us that they never had any intention of being slaves in Egypt. After all, they were God's special people. Not because they were any better than anybody else but because God just chose them. Genesis 12:1-3 relates how this choice got started.

The LORD had said to Abram, "Leave your country, your people and your father's household and go to the land I will show you. I will make you into a great nation and I will bless you; I will make your name great, and you will be a blessing. I will bless those who bless you, and whoever curses you I will curse; and all peoples on earth will be blessed through you."

Abram (who later became Abraham) was the father of Isaac, and Isaac was the father of Jacob. Jacob's name was later changed to Israel, and his descendents are called the Israelites. God had promised to make Abraham's descendents a great nation, and He is fulfilling His promise in the Israelites. God could have chosen any group of people, but He chose the descendents of Abram because He's God and He can do whatever He wants to do.

God has always had a heart for fellowship with humans, His highest creation. He wants to communicate His love to us since those first walks in the garden with Adam, but we consistently and stubbornly turn from sweet fellowship with God to seek more thrills. How we can imagine anything better than what God has for us is inconceivable, yet we do it, don't we? Like Eve, we figure God must be keeping something from us. Remember the serpent's deceptive ploy? "For God knows that when you eat of it your eyes will be opened, and you will be like God, knowing good and evil" (Gen. 3:5).

It was true that when she ate the fruit, Eve would know good from evil. The point is, Eve had only known good. God was trying to protect her from experiencing evil. But what did Eve decide to do?

When the woman saw that the fruit of the tree was good for food and pleasing to the eye, and also desirable for gaining wisdom, she took some and ate it. She also gave some to her husband, who was with her, and he ate it. Then the eyes of both of them were opened, and they realized they were naked; so they sewed fig leaves together and made coverings for themselves *(vv. 6-7).*

So bite-bite-chew-chew, Adam joins in, and there went their innocence, their spiritual lives, and the spiritual lives of the babies of the future. (Thanks a lot, you two!)

Now God kicks the plan into play to communicate His love to humankind another way. As the descendents of Adam and Eve multiplied into the nation of Israel, I believe His thoughts toward them went something like this: "You are going to have all these special laws. You're going to be different, so that people will ask you, 'Why are you different?' Then you can tell them, 'It's the God we serve,' and that's how people are going to get to know Me."

Well, the Israelites got big-headed and began to act as if their reasoning ran something like this, "We're God's chosen people, and we have all these laws, and we do all these different things, because we're special. It's all about us." They totally forgot they weren't God's people because of themselves. They were God's people because of *Him.* They were God's people because of God's purposes, and God's purposes had absolutely nothing to do with any attributes they might have possessed.

So God moved to get their attention. Being God, He was already two steps ahead of them. God had told Abraham years before that his descendents would have to endure slavery. "And he said unto Abram, Know of a surety that thy seed shall be a stranger in a land that is not theirs, and shall serve them; and they shall afflict them four hundred years; and also that nation, whom they shall serve, will I judge: and afterward shall they come out with great substance" (Gen. 15:13-14, KJV).

This time of slavery served both as a reason for God to judge Egypt and a rebuke on Israel. Funny how hardship has a way of suddenly getting our attention! The Israelites never intended to be slaves in Egypt, but there they were, and there was nothing to do but survive and look to God in hope of deliverance.

The decades passed. Generations were born and died. The Israelites got used to being slaves. Even though they hoped for a deliverer, they lived through the experience, slowly developing a slave mentality because their will was being broken. They hated their situation but were forced to adjust to it. Do you know anybody like that?

My friends and I just shook our heads in wonder that God put up with us and still loved us enough to sustain us through what we jokingly called our own "Egyptian periods." Like the Israelites, each of us had sojourned—or was presently sojourning—in Egypt. Our Egypts took the form of stressful relationships, problems with children, financial struggles, and so on. And while in the midst of our issues— like the Israelites in the midst of their bondage—we became accustomed to the language, the landscape, the attitudes, and even the food. We hadn't planned to, but we became Egyptized. We realized that the longer we stayed in Egypt, the more Egyptian we became. Some of us had picked up the accent, others learned the idioms and hand gestures, still others adopted the dress and makeup styles, and some exhibited the attitudes.

For example, Heather (not her real name) had been a promiscuous teenager. She had a great relationship with her parents, but her natural, adolescent sexual curiosity was met with disapproving responses from her well-intentioned mother. Her loving father was emotionally shy and virtually silent about the subject of her relationship with boys. The way her parents dealt with the topic actually fueled her need for responses from the opposite sex. Left to her own devices, she fulfilled that need inappropriately by becoming sexually active by the time she was 16.

By 18, when Heather received Christ into her heart as her Savior, her spiritual needs began to be met, but she had not learned how to fulfill her emotional needs in holy ways. She continually fought the habit she learned in her own Egypt of satisfying her emotional needs by participating in sexual relationships with boys.

As my girlfriends and I continued to talk, we realized it didn't really matter how we got to our individual Egypts—our own choices, pure chance, others' choices, childhood abuse, neglect, ignorance, or just blatant disobedience—the result is always the same. We, like the Israelites—despite their hatred of all things Egyptian—have developed a fondness for the food. With those taste buds awakened, we craved the things we were accustomed to but were never born to enjoy. We were connoisseurs of Egyptian delights. (Of course, by now you realize that by Egypt I mean "the world"—those ways that are contrary to God's ways.) Becoming connoisseurs was the Israelites' first mistake—a mistake they didn't even know they were making.

We were all in Egypt before our relationship with God. However, like my friends and me, maybe you're a Christian who took a side trip to Egypt. However it went for you, you now find yourself with tastes and cravings that are opposite to what pleases God.

## Adapting or Adopting

Know this: There's a difference between adapting to your situation and adopting it. It's possible to be in the midst of struggles and adapt to them without adopting them forever. Christians who have joy in the midst of their trials have *adapted* without adopting the negative effects of those trials. How do you know if you adapted or adopted?

You know by how you think and act when separated from the trial or issue. If you respond with the same attitudes and reactions that you had during the trial, you have *adopted* its effects.

While in Egypt, the Israelites adopted some of the ways of the Egyptians. How do we know that? Look at what they said and did when they got out of Egypt. They were delivered and crossed the Red Sea, but the first little problem that came up found them crying—not for comfort from the God who had just delivered them—but for the things Egypt had supplied.

> The whole Israelite community set out from Elim . . . on the fifteenth day of the second month after they had come out of Egypt. In the desert the whole community grumbled against Moses and Aaron. The Israelites said to them, "If only we had died by the LORD's hand in Egypt! There we sat around pots of meat and ate all the food we wanted, but you have brought us out into this desert to starve this entire assembly to death" *(Exod. 16:1-3).*

Even after God began to supply them *literally* with bread from heaven, what they craved was what they had in Egypt. "We remember the fish, which we did eat in Egypt freely; the cucumbers, and the melons, and the leeks, and the onions, and the garlick: But now our soul is dried away: there is nothing at all, beside this manna, before our eyes" (Num. 11:5-6, KJV).

Why did the Israelites grumble so much? They had been freed from their bondage—their Egypt—and were headed to the land God described as a place flowing with milk and honey. "And I am come down to deliver them out of the hand of the Egyptians, and to bring them up out of that land unto a good land and a large, unto a land flowing with milk and honey" (Exod. 3:8, KJV).

What moved them to keep looking back? They had developed an Egyptian taste while they lived where they had no intention of being in the first place.

## Yummy—Leeks and Onions

You're the same way. You've been in Egypt. You've also adopted some Egyptian tastes. But now you've crossed your Red Sea—you've become a Christian or you've rededicated your life to Christ—and you are trying to cross over into your Promised Land. The minute you enter, you will be able to partake of milk and honey, the diet of Promised Land dwellers. The problem is, you still crave leeks and onions.

No one ever said leeks and onions don't taste good, but you are not supposed to dine on leeks and onions in the Promised Land. That's slavery food, but that's all you know. So what do you do? You try to make leeks and onions compatible with milk and honey. You try mixing new recipes. But no matter what you do, you can't get those leeks and onions to blend with milk and honey. Until you develop a completely new taste for milk and honey, you will not get the taste of leeks and onions out of your mouth.

Throughout the rest of this book I am going to challenge you to come to grips with the leeks-and-onions issues in your life. If you don't want to be confronted, you may as well stop reading this book right now and give it to someone who is serious about making a change.

But I think you really want to live a milk-and-honey life. I believe you desire a transformation because you realize that the way things are going is not working for you. I'm suggesting that you start renovating your tastes by taking a long, hard look back to see how you got to this place in your life. I contend that once you understand that, you can begin to experience the milk-and-honey life.

# Two

# Location

## How Did I End Up Here?

So here you are, ready to cross into the Promised Land. You are a Christian, but you've internalized some of the world's tastes and outlooks. The problem with this is that your tastes have conditioned you to look, act, and react to issues just like a non-Christian would. No wonder your issues are beating you down. It's said that insanity is doing the same thing in the same old way and expecting a different result. Are you doing things the same way, getting the same bad results, and wondering why you're still failing? You will not move toward the goal God has for you until you recognize where you are and point yourself in the direction He wants you to go. Until you admit that change must start with you, there will be little progress.

Let me tell you about the string of boyfriends from my past. It's not that these men were not decent individuals; they were. The problem was, I was looking for a husband, but I was choosing men who were not husband material. The common denominator? Commitment phobia. They were all fun-loving but needy. There were lots of laughs, but I was working hard to fulfill their needs without reciprocation. Eventually, each relationship ended.

It finally dawned on me. They weren't the problem. I was the problem. These men lived their lives just the way they wanted to. I was the one wanting more from the relationship. I accepted it because I received a measure of satisfaction by fulfilling their neediness. Then, when I didn't get what I wanted from the relationship, I was hurt. I blamed them for acting in accordance with their character.

I had to get my thinking in the right place, and I had to turn my attention to the right places. In other words, I had to realize my *location* in life—and make the decision to change *me* if I hoped to see different results.

Location is all-important. Look at our current business climate. When a business looks to make a lot of money, the saying is "Location, location, location." It's all about where you place your store or yourself. Being in the right place will make a lot of difference in the way things turn out. You hear people say it all the time: "I was in the right place at the right time." Conversely, being in the wrong place at the wrong time has a huge impact on our lives too. Much of our physical, mental, and emotional health is determined not by what we have or haven't done but by where we are. The Israelites' problem was directly related to where they were—in Egypt. We dwell in our own Egypts attitudinally, and by virtue of where we are, we have certain problems.

Have you ever noticed that embarrassing or unexpected things always seem to happen when you are somewhere you have no business being in the first place? My most embarrassing moment happened in just such a circumstance.

During my late teens and early 20s, I was on the dating scene. Some of the guys I dated I really had no business being around for various reasons. One of those guys was a captain in the Marine Corps. One day he invited me to visit him at Camp Pendleton. He was the Officer of the Day at a particular post, and we planned to have lunch together. I drove through a fast-food joint, purchased our hamburgers and sodas, and headed for the base in my silver RX7 with the sunroof open. Now you know you can't drive a sports car sans sunroof without attitude, and I certainly had it going on.

I went through all the checkpoints and finally found the building where my friend worked. I pulled my silver sports car into a space right near the flagpole. The men who worked under his leadership tried to sneak a peek at me through the large plate-glass windows to see the captain's girlfriend. Knowing I was being watched made me pretty self-conscious. I got out of the car, leaned in to get the food, and balancing everything ever so gingerly, I moved with my most ladylike gait up the sidewalk to the entrance. The men let me in the door and directed me around a corner and down a long hallway to the captain's office.

If you know anything about a Marine Corps base, you know that everything is spit-shined. Nothing was different that day. The long hallway was freshly waxed. I made it about four steps down the hall, and BAM! Down I went, smack on my rear end. Fries and soda flew in every direction. I wanted the floor to open and swallow me.

Four well-toned, burly Marines rushed from behind the reception desk, assisted me up, and tried their best to help me preserve my dignity. They didn't laugh in front of me, probably because my captain friend emerged from his office, barking sharp rebukes at them for "letting her fall." My vindication was short-lived, though. As soon as I was safely in his office, he doubled over in laughter himself.

I wouldn't have that story to tell if I had been doing what I was supposed to do in the first place—leaving non-Christian men alone. My relationship with that guy didn't last too long because I discovered there was something very unsavory about his lifestyle. I had no business dating him in the first place. I was with him because I had developed a taste for the wrong kind of guy.

Examine your taste in friends and in men you date.

List the qualities you find most favorable in the people with whom you socialize.

List the qualities of someone who is following God.

Do these two lists match up?

Does one of the lists make you think of leeks and onions?

Does one of the lists make you think of milk and honey?

King David, the man after God's own heart, was where he had no business being when he got into the Bathsheba incident. Read the story for yourself in 2 Sam. 11:1-4. It says David was at home "at the time when kings go forth to battle" (v. 1, KJV). What did that say? "At the time when kings go forth to battle . . . David tarried still at Jerusalem . . . [and he] arose from off his bed, and walked upon the roof of the king's house" (vv. 1-2, KJV).

Why was David home? If he had been at the battle, he wouldn't have gotten into trouble. He was where he shouldn't have been. And why was Bathsheba bathing on the roof in full view of the palace? I don't know, but I have a suspicion she knew the king was home. Anyway, there he was and there she was. Somewhere along the line, someone was where he or she was not supposed to be, and the result was trouble.

When we are in the wrong place, trouble isn't far away. Sometimes we run headlong into trouble because we fail to consider possible consequences of our actions. In these situations, we did not ask God for direction. He did not lead us into the trouble. And while we are where we shouldn't be, we are vulnerable to develop tastes for the wrong things.

God loves us but will not violate our will. Even though He does have some very persuasive ways of getting our attention (remember Jonah), it is still up to us to respond positively when He calls. The longer we stay in the wrong place, the harder it will be to tear ourselves away.

So ask yourself: *What is my location and where am I supposed to be?*

I was a Christian woman pursuing a speaking and writing career when I found myself divorced, bankrupt, homeless, and a single mother. I had to take a hard look at my life.

I wasn't where I planned to be, and I wasn't where I wanted to be. But I was God's child, and I was in His hands.

I needed to become aware of my location. As long as I was worried, and trying to work things out on my own, God couldn't work. I sensed God was waiting for me to settle down and seek His direction in my life.

Like me, you belong to the God of the universe. And He is there with you through bankruptcy, divorce, an unplanned pregnancy, a spot on the X ray, a wayward child, and every difficulty you can think of—even difficulties of your own making.

## Evaluate Your Location

I believe you are in one of four basic locations today. Look them over, and if you agree, pinpoint where you are today.

### Location 1: All Is Well

You got to where you are today through careful prayer and exercising spiritual wisdom. Things are going well for you. Hallelujah! You are in the position to be a prayer support for the rest of us. Ask God to give you insight into the struggles your friends face and ask Him to show you ways He wants to use you to minister to them. This is also a season of life He will use to prepare you for future struggles you may face.

### Location 2: Unexpected Outcomes

You chose this location, but some unexpected things have happened, and you've had to deal with some surprises. You may now regret your choice, feeling sorry you made it, or may even be trying to find a way out of your situation.

### Location 3: Suffering the Consequences of Poor Choices

This may be the most discouraging location because it is the consequence of your own poor choices. You may feel like beating yourself up or giving up. You are in serious need of relief.

## Location 4: A Place You Did Not Choose

You find yourself in a life situation that was thrust upon you. Even though it is not a result of your choices, you must deal with it. You may feel stuck and resentful, or you may believe that this is your lot in life and nothing will ever make you feel better.

Take a few moments to evaluate your present location.

What dominates your thoughts and emotions? _____

Rate your satisfaction with the following areas of your life on a scale of 1 to 10, with 10 being completely satisfied and 1 being totally dissatisfied.

Spiritual growth ____

Relationships ____

Emotions ____

Physical body ____

My current location in life is a result of: (check one)

My choice(s) ____

Pure chance ____

Someone else's choice ____

Some combination of choice and chance ____

Since I took stock of my location some time back, I haven't done everything right, but I have constantly reminded myself that I am in God's hands, not flailing about on my own. I try to live as a listener and say as Saul (later Paul) said in Acts 9:6 (NKJV), "Lord, what do You want me to do?" I didn't plan for the hard things that have happened in my life so far, but God has helped me learn and grow through those difficult times. And guess what! Those times have driven me to rely on Him in ways I never did before.

God has helped me deal with uncertainty, embarrassment, and shame. He's helped me face and make new decisions about things I didn't expect to deal with. At times, I have been forced to renovate my comfort zone. God has graciously allowed me to learn through the process. Above and beyond my personal trials, I've learned that lots of folks have the problems I've experienced. And, wonder of wonders—the women to whom I minister know these same struggles. I'm even aware that some of you could hear the specific struggles of my life and think it's a piece of cake compared to what is happening in yours. The point is that God spoke to my heart after walking with me through months of struggle.

"Sharon," He whispered, "now that you have learned to depend on Me, you can tell other ladies that it's possible. You always believed I was there for you, but it was a head-only belief. Now your belief is grounded both in My truth and in your experiences. Encourage My daughters. Tell them they can make it too."

No matter what the predicament, God walks with us through every rough spot. God loves His children no matter where we are in life, and He will stick with us and lead us through it.

Where do you sense God is leading you right now?

Jot down your thoughts about this in a prayer to God. Keep this for later reference as you work through this book.

The Israelites did not plan to end up in Egyptian captivity, but the choice was not theirs. God needed His people to be in one place at one time so He could use them for His special purpose.

God intended for His people to possess the Promised Land. It would take an army to do that. Look at the way it worked out.

There was no way Abraham and Isaac alone could overthrow the people living on the land destined to be the Promised Land. The population had to grow. So Isaac had Jacob and Esau. Still not enough. Jacob had 12 sons and each of those sons had sons. Still not enough. If they had been allowed to stay out in the free world, it's very possible these descendants of Abraham would intermarry with women of other cultural beliefs and their godly heritage would be inextricably lost.

So God placed them in a situation that made intermarriage virtually impossible. First, the small, still-intact family of Jacob (Israel), those original 12 sons and their families, moved to Goshen, Egypt's best land. The cultural difference was so profound that they had no problem marrying within their own culture, and their population grew rapidly.

I'm not saying it is necessary to remain racially separate today. The only stipulation that existed biblically forbidding intermarriage was on the basis of religious belief. We see from the stories of Rahab the harlot of Jericho and Ruth the Moabitess that God did not hate people who were technically described as heathen. In fact, both of these women married into an Israelite family and both ended up in the genealogy of Jesus Christ.

Then "there arose up a new king over Egypt, which knew not Joseph" (Exod. 1:8, KJV; see vv. 6-14). The king's concern regarding these foreigners in his land was directly related to the size of their population. This new Pharaoh forced them into slavery because he was afraid that if they joined with his enemies the new alliance would be large and powerful enough to overthrow him.

Slavery further isolated the Israelites, ensuring that they would marry within their station. Marriage between a slave and a free Egyptian would be virtually unheard of—extremely taboo.

Despite the rigors of slavery, however, the Israeli population continued to grow. Pharaoh's attempts to stem the growth failed. Enter Moses.

It took 10 progressively devastating plagues before Pharaoh was persuaded to let the Israelites go. And when Moses rounded up the people to lead them out of Egypt and away from their hard lives of slavery, conservative estimates set the number of people between 600,000 and 2 million. Quite an army, wouldn't you say?

The Israelites did not plan to be in Egypt. They were there by God's design. They still should not have developed and adopted tastes for Egyptian delights. In God's economy, stuff can happen either way. Situations arise because we did not prevent them, or God may engineer situations for our ultimate good. Where we are *physically* should have absolutely no bearing upon where we are *spiritually*.

Make a list of all the things you plan to accomplish and the places you plan to go within the next 1 year, 5 years, and 10 years.

Now make another list of all the things and places you plan to avoid within the next 1 year, 5 years, and 10 years.

Write down how you plan to accomplish your goals on both lists.

Submit the lists to God in prayer.

## Three

# Perception
## What Can I Understand About Myself?

Recently, I met a lovely woman while at a family gathering
out of town. Debra and I struck up a conversation and
clicked immediately, becoming fast friends. We soon found
that we had been through similar past hurts, which helped
us bond even more.

When I began to explain the premise of this book (I was
in the midst of writing this chapter when we met), Debra
shared with me that it wasn't until recently that she began
to really understand herself. As the fourth child of 13 children, she grew up in a crowd, sharing, compromising, and
helping to raise her younger siblings. There just wasn't
room or time for being her own person.

At the age of 16, Debra gave birth to her first child, got
married, and before she was 20, she was mother to three
toddlers. Again there was no time to think of herself.

When her marriage fell apart, it was all Debra could do
just to survive one day at a time. After her second marriage
ended in divorce, she decided to ask God if there was something He could tell her about her situation. Was there something He might want to communicate to her about herself?
Why was she making the choices she was making?

Now over 50, and after much prayer and ongoing study
of God's Word, Debra has reached a level of understanding
about herself she never had before. For one thing, she real-
izes the choices she made were a result of her own neediness and low self-esteem. She had also lived for everyone

else for so long she didn't even know her own favorite color, favorite foods, or other personal preferences.

What do you understand about yourself? Take a clue from Debra. Now that you have discovered your location in the last chapter, take time to delve more deeply into each one.

# Location 1: All Is Well

Imagine the excitement of the Israelites on the morning following the final plague. After being startled awake and forced to begin their journey, I'm sure they were still psyched as the sun began to rise. Moreover, on top of gaining their freedom, add the rush of spoiling the Egyptians, who in their panic and fear had thrown riches at their now ex-slaves hoping to gain a little favor before they all ended up dead. The Bible describes it this way:

> And it came to pass, that at midnight the LORD smote all the firstborn in the land of Egypt, from the firstborn of Pharaoh that sat on his throne unto the firstborn of the captive that was in the dungeon; and all the firstborn of cattle. And Pharaoh rose up in the night, he, and all his servants, and all the Egyptians; and there was a great cry in Egypt; for there was not a house where there was not one dead. . . . And the Egyptians were urgent upon the people, that they might send them out of the land in haste; for they said, We be all dead men. . . . And the LORD gave the people favour in the sight of the Egyptians, so that they lent unto them such things as they required. And they spoiled the Egyptians (*Exod. 12:29-30, 33, 36, KJV*).

There must be few things that feel better than your first day of freedom. Troubles are behind; nothing but blue skies lie ahead. That's the feeling of the all-is-well location. Some mornings I awaken in this location. There are no aches and pains, my family is safe, my husband loves me, I have a satisfying job, and we received no emergency calls in the night.

If you are in the all-is-well location and everything is going fine in your life right now, you have two specific responsibilities to keep you focused on milk-and-honey pursuits. Your social responsibility is to encourage others. Your personal responsibility is to be vigilant in your own spiritual development.

## Social Responsibility: Encourage

Even after the children of Israel had been in the Promised Land for some time, they were still having a tough go. Thanks to their own refusal to remain dedicated to God, He allowed them to be repeatedly subjugated under the thumb of enemy kings. Deborah, a prophetess, judged Israel during a time when King Jabin of Canaan terrorized her people. To add to her work dealing with the people's problems, Barak, the Israelite army's captain, refused to lead Israel's fighters against Jabin's captain, Sisera, unless Deborah went with him. (See Judg. 4.)

You may be wondering why I've chosen Deborah as someone in the all-is-well location. Looks like the times of her life were pretty tough. I suppose that's one way of looking at her. But I see Deborah in the all-is-well location because she was living her life and doing her God-given job effectively enough that she was available to help her friend. Despite outside social circumstances, her life was so in order that she was not overburdened or too wrapped up in herself to be there when Barak needed her.

Romans 12:15-16 says, "Rejoice with those who rejoice; mourn with those who mourn. Live in harmony with one another. Do not be proud, but be willing to associate with people of low position. Do not be conceited." When all is well, there's more time to function outside of yourself.

Since your own situation is in order, you can commit to creative ways to rejoice in the joys and accomplishments of others and to comfort those who are in trouble or in grief.

In all our busyness these days, lots can be said for just slowing down long enough to simply spend time with each other. When did you last attend an event for the pure enjoyment of it without having someplace else to rush off to? Besides church, how often do you attend a function where you turn your cell phone off?

With whom do you need to spend time?

Jot his or her name down in your organizer or PDA and schedule a time to make contact.

Schedule a meeting such as tea at your house, lunch, dinner, or a shopping excursion, then do it.

I recently had an opportunity to be an encouragement for one of my friends. We had not seen each other for more than seven years when Alexis (not her real name) and I bumped into each other in the elevator of a parking garage on our way to a jazz concert. We were ecstatic to see each other again, but both our lives had changed a lot. Fifteen years earlier we had been young brides planning our weddings. Now we were attending a jazz concert with men who were not those grooms. As Ricky Ricardo would have said to

Lucy, we "had some 'splainin' to do." We agreed to be in touch the next day to set up dinner the following week.

My divorce had been finalized years earlier. God had weaved counseling, prayer, and time into the safety net that cushioned my fall through the separation and final full split. He eventually guided me into the heart of my new, wonderful husband James, and once again, all was well.

That tedious journey, one I never intended to take, sensitized me to the emotional upheaval divorce can produce. Sitting across from Alexis in the restaurant, her smile, her perfectly coifed hair, and her business suit said, "All's well," but her eyes screamed her pain. The kindred connection was electric and immediate.

Alexis began to share that her husband's infidelity, his unrepentant heart, and her church's lack of disciplinary action toward him—a deacon—had combined to cause the divorce. She now dated occasionally, but the recovery was hard.

I listened, empathized, and loved her. Our busy schedules leave us little time, but I am determined to carve some time out just for us every so often. God is allowing me to use my past pain to walk through this valley with Alexis. It is my social responsibility.

When all is well for me and I take the time to encourage someone else, that's milk-and-honey living.

## Personal Responsibility: Be Vigilant in Your Own Spiritual Development

Your personal responsibility in the all-is-well location is to be vigilant. While some of your time should be spent encouraging others, be sure to focus quality attention on your own spiritual development. Just how should you go about it?

When in the all-is-well location, it's easy to fall into a false sense of security and thus slip back into craving or even participating in leeks-and-onions pleasures. Smooth seas rock you to sleep. Then, once you're slumbering, your ship drifts far from shore, a storm comes up, and the waves overwhelm and capsize your vessel. You end up under dark clouds even though you started out under clear skies. Why? Because you weren't paying attention. You slept while the storm clouds gathered.

Remaining alert can be complicated. Think about driving a car. Your main objective when you drive is to progress from point A to point B. To do so, you drive a vehicle equipped with three mirrors that allow you to look behind you. What possible reason could there be to look back when the objective is to move forward? You look back to have a full and complete view of the road and other drivers. Something may be gaining on you or attempting to pass you just as you change lanes. It's only in repeatedly looking back and evaluating what you see that you successfully move forward.

To safely reach your destination, you must watch the road in front, check the rearview mirrors, turn to check the blind spots, watch the dials or digits on the dashboard, and negotiate your turns. To all this, you probably add playing the radio or a CD, dealing with a passenger (which could mean breaking up the kids' fight), and talking on your cell phone (using a hands-free earpiece, of course). I hope you're not like the woman my husband saw applying make-up, drinking coffee, and reading a book while driving!

Vigilance is no less complicated in your spiritual life. Although necessary in every circumstance, in the all-is-well location, vigilance acts as body-building exercises. What you pay attention to now will make you strong and will be your reserve spiritual muscle when your location changes.

We are instructed in 1 Pet. 5:6-9 with two prerequisites, one prompt, and two purposes for vigilance.

## *Prerequisites*

The first prerequisite to vigilance is humility. "Humble yourselves therefore under the mighty hand of God, that he may exalt you in due time" (v. 6, KJV).

It is God who is able to give you wisdom and insight. Submit to Him to increase your own understanding. Humble yourself before Him. Let your heart soften to His voice. Rest in His hand, gaze into His face, and listen to what He has to say to you. He'll speak through your reading of His Word, prayer, and hearing from other saints. Then you'll experience the incredible lifting that only God can do.

It may seem odd, but the way to be lifted up is by becoming humble. That's really not so hard to understand. Have you ever needed a leg up in order to peek over a wall or fence? What did you do? You asked someone for a boost. Your friend then locked his or her fingers together and offered his or her attached palms for your foot so you could be hoisted up to see. You had to trust your friend, submit to your friend's strength, and humble yourself to be held up in order to be lifted higher. Then you were able to see. You did not see what you needed to see until you surrendered to your friend.

This is how humility functions before God as a necessity for vigilance. You will not see what you must see until you humbly allow God to lift you to the necessary vantage point.

The second prerequisite to vigilance is the necessity to cast your cares on God. "Cast all your anxiety on him because he cares for you" (v. 7).

My youngest son plays basketball. I watch the team warm up before the games. Some of the players wear sweats, some have on jewelry, and others wear small wrist weights. They shoot around on the court and stretch along the sidelines. However, before they start the game, they peel off the sweats, remove the jewelry, and abandon the wrist weights. Why? They need to be as light and free as possible to run swiftly up and down that court and jump high for those baskets and rebounds. If they kept all those encumbrances on, they'd be more concerned with them than with the game.

It's the same with the concerns of your life and mine. We will not be vigilant if we're filled with anxiety. We can't look up and out if we are looking in.

Allow God to take care of your cares. You do believe He can handle things better than you can, don't you? Even when all is well, the cares of the world will try to sneak in and steal your joy. The minute you recognize the encroachment, toss those concerns right into God's hands so you can be vigilant about what God would have you to be vigilant about.

What are you stubbornly refusing to let God handle?


Let it go.

Pray now and refuse to take it back.


*Prompt*

Once those of you in the all-is-well location have humbled yourselves and cast your cares on God, you are prompted to be sober. This word *sober* is translated from a Greek word meaning "moderate, discreet, and sane." To be sober is to abstain from any kind of excess. This is the same word used in Titus 2 to counsel young men who tend to disregard consequences and to caution young women who would dress too extravagantly or speak without thinking. It's also the same word used in 1 Tim. 3:2 to discuss the importance of a minister's judgment and conduct.

The simple two-word phrase in 1 Pet. 5:8 offers itself as

the necessary prompt preceding vigilance. It is absolutely crucial to be in control of yourself to be successfully vigilant. The opposite of sobriety is inebriation, and none of us would feel safe if police officers, security guards, and soldiers tried to discharge their duties while inebriated. We know they would not be in full control of their faculties. Lawbreakers and enemies could overrun them and chaos would ensue. Inebriation causes one to act wild, move erratically, and think irrationally. Individuals are in no condition to be watchful when not sober.

Have you noticed that once weights are lifted off it's easy to get reencumbered? As soon as you're out of debt, you feel as though you have lots of money, so you start buying lots of things again and end up right back in debt. As soon as you clear your schedule, you feel like you have lots of time, so you fill it up and before you know it you're overbooked again. Operating soberly will allow you to think things through before you make rash decisions or poor choices and will help you distinguish between leeks-and-onions decisions and milk-and-honey decisions.

The prompt that says, "Be sober," leads us directly to the command itself that instructs us to "be vigilant." The abolitionist Wendell Phillips said, "Eternal vigilance is the price of liberty." In other words, we cannot even experience or maintain freedom unless we stay attentive. We cannot understand and properly function in our position in the all-is-well location without being vigilant. Bad things happen when we are not paying attention.

### Purposes

Both purposes and reasons for being vigilant are found in 1 Pet. 5:8-9: "Be sober, be vigilant; because your adversary the devil, as a roaring lion, walketh about, seeking whom he may devour: whom resist stedfast in the faith, knowing that the same afflictions are accomplished in your brethren that are in the world" (KJV).

The first purpose for vigilance is devil resistance. You must be on the alert for the tricks of the devil. As this verse says, the devil is your adversary, your enemy, and it would bring him nothing but pleasure to completely destroy you. But notice, you will be able to know when he's coming because he's roaring. His tactics are not secrets. In Cor. 2:11 it is stated, "Lest Satan should get an advantage of us: for we are not ignorant of his devices" (KJV). If you're vigilant, if you're watching, you will see Satan's approach. If you're vigilant, if you're listening, you will hear Satan's approach.

Pay attention. Satan still tempts by attacking your flesh, your eyes, or your pride. In Gen. 3:6, Eve "saw that the tree was good for food, and that it was pleasant to the eyes, and a tree to be desired to make one wise" (KJV). Do you see it? He went after her flesh (good for food), her eyes (pleasant to the eyes), and her pride (desired to make one wise). Eve knew that she wasn't supposed to eat from that tree. This is how Satan roars.

Like Eve, you already know what's right. When you doubt along the lines of your flesh, your eyes, or your pride, that's Satan's roar. When in doubt, don't.

We give Eve a hard time, but let's be honest, ladies. We are still easily deceived by Satan's same roar. Get a little lonely and let an ex-boyfriend slide back into the picture, saying all the right things, and pow! We're putty. Been there; done that. The man floated back into my life, my flesh stirred, my eyes saw how dignified the gray at his temples made him look, and when his eyes twinkled my way, my pride screamed, "Girl, you've still got it!"

I bit, and like Eve, immediately my eyes were opened. I knew evil and how devastated I was to discover that the evil was within me. I had not stayed alert, and the shame was a true death experience.

How are you being tempted by what you see?



How is your flesh being tempted?



What is your pride pulling you to do?



The second purpose for vigilance is empathy. Watchfulness allows you to realize that other people are going through the same thing. This can be understood two ways. First, your vigilance can allow you to see how others are handling the situations that have not yet come your way. You will be able to steer clear. For example, I don't need to snort cocaine to know its bad for me. All I need to do is look at an addict to understand I don't want to be where he or she is.

Second, your vigilance will allow you to empathize with people who are going through things you've faced. You will be able to identify and be there for the person if he or she needs an understanding ear. Remember my friend Alexis? Because I worked through my issues with God's help, my vigilance helped me remember what He taught me so that I could help her over that same hump.

The all-is-well location is wonderful, but it is filled with responsibility. Be thankful that God has you in such a wonderful place in your life, and bring Him glory by encouraging others and remaining vigilant.

# Location 2: Unexpected Outcomes

Perhaps you can't say that all is well in your life right now. That's just not the location you are in. Look again at the Israelites as a group of people able to identify with you if you are in Location 2—facing a situation you thought would turn out differently.

The Israelites knew what they were moving *from* when they left Egypt, but I don't think they had a clue what they were moving *to*. We're not told much about the overall exit plan other than the fact that they were all supposed to leave Egypt. How was Moses expected to feed all those people? Who was initially in charge of sleeping arrangements and bathroom breaks? The exit was indeed necessary, but then what?

These thoughts undoubtedly floated through the minds of the Israelites too. At their first stop after the crossing of the Red Sea, they panicked. What was happening was not what they expected. "Then Moses led Israel from the Red Sea and they went into the Desert of Shur. For three days they traveled in the desert without finding water. When they came to Marah, they could not drink its water because it was bitter. (That is why the place is called Marah.) So the people grumbled against Moses, saying, 'What are we to drink?'" (Exod. 15:22-24).

Now in our wisdom, it's pretty easy to say, "They should have had no problem. God was in complete control. He wouldn't have told Moses to go get all those people if He didn't have a plan for caring for them. Hadn't they just seen God send 10 incredibly devastating plagues on the Egyptians? Hadn't they just witnessed God do the impossible by bringing Pharaoh to his knees? All they needed to do was trust God. Everything would be OK."

Good comeback. Then why don't we follow that wise advice ourselves? We find ourselves in Location 2 when we have made choices we believe are right and smart, when we know we've heard from God, when we know we've seen God move, yet things have gone awry. We end up faced with outcomes we did not expect. The correct thing to do is keep trusting God. We believed Him when we made the initial choices. The tough part comes when we face the challenge. How do we continue believing Him when things don't seem to be going our way?

Ruth faced that exact dilemma. She married a Jewish fellow and accepted his God as her own. That's two big changes at once. I remember the excitement of being a new bride, basking in the glow of my new husband's love, and itching to tell my love story to anyone who would listen. I also remember the exhilaration of being a new Christian, basking in the glow of the Savior's love and grace, and zealous to announce to the world His availability for them too. Ruth had both of these sensations happening within her at the same time. She had to be sitting on top of the world emotionally.

Then disaster struck. Her father-in-law, brother-in-law, and beloved new husband all died. What was this? She had just begun learning to trust this new God. Everything had been perfect. Ruth may have thought about giving up and going back to her old life, but we have no scriptural indication of that. Naomi, her mother-in-law, pressed her to return to her own family, Ruth sternly retorted, "Intreat me not to leave thee . . . for whither thou goest, I will go; and where thou lodgest, I will lodge: thy people shall be my people, and thy God my God: where thou diest, will I die, and there will I be buried: the LORD do so to me, and more also, if ought but death part thee and me" (Ruth 1:16-17, KJV).

Ruth chose what we must choose—to keep trusting God

no matter what. Circumstances change; God does not. God has promised to take care of you. That's why you can say, like Paul, "I have learned to be content whatever the circumstances" (Phil. 4:11).

Look up the following verses and write down how they speak to the point just made that God can be trusted even when things don't go as planned.

Mal. 3:6

Heb. 13:5

So, in Location 2, when you have chosen wisely but you are experiencing unexpected outcomes, here are two practical responses: Don't worry, and get dressed.

### Don't Worry

It's so easy to say "Don't worry," when you have nothing to worry about, isn't it? I can hear your heart screaming, "How, Sharon? How exactly am I supposed to just not think about the rotten way things are going?"

The Word of God never said don't think about it. You're human, and you're not stupid or detached from reality. You will notice your situation. In fact, you will and you should remain acutely aware of what's going on around you. What the Word says is don't worry about it.

There's a huge difference between knowing about a situation and worrying about it. I know that there are bills to pay for the household every month, but I don't worry about them. Why? Because my husband handles our bills. That's his job and he's good at it. My employment doesn't pay enough to cover all those bills anyway, so it would be pointless for me to wring my hands in anxiety over our household bills.

It's the same with a problem you may be facing. The problem is so big that your limited resources can't solve it. You have someone in your life, though, who can. God. God can handle the issues of your life. And He's good at it too.

Your first response in Location 2 must be "I will not worry."

Use Phil. 4:6-7 as a prayer model that can be paraphrased and personalized to your situation something like this:

God, I refuse to worry about ___(problem)___. I am coming to You in prayer, asking You to handle ___(problem)___. I am thanking You already for taking care of ___(problem)___. I gladly accept Your peace about ___(problem)___, although I don't fully understand it. I surrender my heart and my mind and allow them to be enveloped by the peace You have provided to me through Jesus Christ.

### Get Dressed

Your second response while in Location 2 is to get dressed in the armor of God. Now you should always have on this suit, but it's especially necessary to remind yourself of the armor when facing circumstances that could knock you off your feet.

Remember, Location 2 is a place where God has allowed you to land even though you prayerfully sought His guidance beforehand. You didn't choose haphazardly or unadvisedly as we will discuss in Location 3. Nor did your situation just happen to you out of the blue, which is Location 4. No, you were deliberate, thoughtful, and obedient. Now things are crazy, and it's not your fault. When faced with unexpected outcomes that threaten to knock you down, the appropriate response—once you remind yourself not to worry—is to remember to suit up for the battle you face.

You have an adversary who seeks to destroy you. Satan absolutely hates it when you operate in the center of God's will. Like he did with Job, he will try to trip you up while you're happily living for the Lord and minding your own business. Read Job 1 and 2:1-10 for the details of Job's story. The armor of God, which is found in Eph. 6, will allow you to withstand Satan's onslaughts. You'll stand as the problem swirls around you.

"Stand therefore, having your loins girt about with truth" (v. 14*a*, KJV).

First, surround yourself with the truth. The best piece of advice I have received so far in life from another human being came from my friend Lanette. While going through a difficult time in my life, I was so stressed by a certain individual's verbal abuse that I became physically weakened to the point of experiencing a collapsed lung. Lanette told me, "Sharon, listen only to what's true."

Those five words changed my life. From then on, every time this person spoke negatively of me, I'd let it roll away and I'd remind myself of the truth about myself. Whenever he'd misjudge our situation, I'd remember what was really going on. When he'd call into question my Christian motives, I'd bring a scripture to mind that reinforced the truth of how I was living.

The truth sets you free (John 8:32). Looking through the spectacles of truth will allow you to see clearly what God wants you to see in your unexpected circumstances of Location 2.

". . . and having on the breastplate of righteousness" (Eph. 6:14*b*).

You won't have a leg to stand on if you abandon righteousness—right living—at a time like this. Unfortunately, it's when circumstances unexpectedly go wrong that we tend to chuck our faith and turn to illegitimate means of comfort or handling the problem. For example, when one relationship is going bad, we jump into another one, thinking that will fix a broken heart. Wrong.

Guard your heart by living righteously before God. Don't lie your way through issues. Refrain from stealing either physical items or another's character. Remain sexually pure. Do not rebel against God's Word. To the contrary, obey diligently so as not to further complicate your life in which unexpected things are already taking place.

"And your feet shod with the preparation of the gospel of peace" (v. 15, KJV).

Keep your testimony alive. You may be thinking, "But things are not going well. I have nothing to testify about." Oh, but you do. Even though it may not seem so, God is still in control. Say so. Acknowledge God's goodness.

From time to time, my friend Mary reminds me of something she remembers about me. She traveled life's road with me through difficult years. She has said she marveled at how I kept going, led chapel services at school, spoke encouragement to other women, and even smiled, although she was well aware of my pain.

Pain or not, difficulty or not, stress or not, one thing I knew—God was still in control. I didn't understand it. I couldn't figure out why this was happening to me, but I knew that no matter how much situations changed, God was with me.

Maintain your testimony. Tell others of God's goodness using your life as an example of one of God's works in progress.

"Above all, taking the shield of faith, wherewith ye shall

be able to quench all the fiery darts of the wicked" (v. 16, KJV).

It's this faith in God alone, even when you don't understand, that will stop Satan dead in his tracks. Faith in God puts out the fire of accusations. Faith in God takes the discouragement out of rejection. Faith in God takes the finality out of failure. Faith in God takes the sting out of death. Nothing Satan can throw at you can harm you when you have faith in God. In times of trouble, don't lose your faith; use your faith.

"And take the helmet of salvation" (v. 17*a*, KJV).

Above all, be sure you have accepted Christ as your Savior. Everything in this book is null and void if you have not received salvation. The words you are reading here are not a magic formula for deliverance from your problems. The words of this book are an offshoot of the words from the ultimate Book to which this volume constantly refers—the Holy Bible. The Bible is the story of God's love, forgiveness, and redemption of humankind back into a relationship with himself through Jesus Christ. If you are not enjoying that relationship with Him, start now.

Read the following verses:

- "For God so loved the world, that he gave his only begotten Son, that whosoever believeth in him should not perish, but have everlasting life" (John 3:16, KJV).
- "For all have sinned, and come short of the glory of God" (Rom. 3:23, KJV).
- "But God commendeth his love toward us, in that, while we were yet sinners, Christ died for us" (5:8, KJV).
- "For the wages of sin is death; but the gift of God is eternal life through Jesus Christ our Lord" (6:23, KJV).
- "That if thou shalt confess with thy mouth the Lord Je-

sus, and shalt believe in thine heart that God hath raised him from the dead, thou shalt be saved. For with the heart man believeth unto righteousness; and with the mouth confession is made unto salvation" (10:9-10, KJV).

If these verses express the desire of your heart, pray through these verses, making them personal. When you finish, thank God for taking up residence in your heart. Welcome to the family of God. You have just been born again!

". . . and the sword of the Spirit, which is the word of God" (Eph. 6:17*b*).

The final piece of the armor is the sword of the Spirit—the Word of God. You will be able to survive to the end of your situation if you use the weapon of the Word. When it's time to fight back, use Scripture.

Jesus did this when He faced Satan. In Matt. 4, Satan was bold enough to tempt Jesus three times. All three times, Jesus answered him with Scripture. We can learn several things from this.

1. Satan is bold. If he tried to trip up Jesus, he'll certainly try it with you.

2. Satan is persistent. One strong answer from Jesus should have shut him up, but it didn't. If he kept needling Jesus, he'll keep needling you.

3. Satan is tricky. Satan used Scripture to try to get Jesus to follow him. We can interpret Scripture accurately, as Jesus did, to keep Satan at bay.

4. Satan is vulnerable. Satan left Jesus for a season when he realized he couldn't win against Him. Satan will leave you, too, for a season when you attack him using God's Word.

As you saw in Job's case and in Ruth's case, God used what happened in their lives as a passageway to a place of purpose. God has somewhere to take you too. Can God trust you to remain faithful to Him even though you are facing circumstances you did not expect?

## Location 3: Suffering the Consequences of Poor Choices

If you are in Location 3, you are suffering the consequences of your own poor choices. This may actually be a more difficult location to be in than the first two. Why? Most of us don't like to be told when we're wrong, and it's even worse when we have to admit the wrong is our own fault.

There are almost too many examples to mention from the lives of the Israelites to show how their poor choices plunged them into negative situations.

- While Moses was communicating face-to-face with God, receiving the Ten Commandments straight from Him, what did the Israelites do? They made a substitute god out of gold and had an orgy in front of it. Poor choice. This made God angry and 3,000 people died as a result. (See Exod. 32:4-6, 28.)

- God led them all the way to the threshold of the Promised Land and they refused to enter. Poor choice. That refusal cost them 40 years of wilderness-wandering during which the entire population of people over 20 years old died except two. (See Num. 32:9-13.)

What is there to do when you find yourself in Location 3? How should you react when you have made poor choices and you now find yourself in a difficult situation?

In 1 Sam. 25, we read about Abigail, a woman who has been where you are. She made an incredibly poor choice when she married Nabal, a man the Bible calls churlish, surly, and wicked. In fact, his name means "fool." Nabal refused to aid David after David's men had been kind to him, so David's anger drove him to prepare to kill Nabal.

Then Abigail heard about the situation. She rushed to prepare a peace offering of sorts and hurried to find David. When she found him, she did things that we, too, should do when faced with the consequences of our poor choices. Abigail acknowledged her poor choice, acted wisely at present despite her poor choice, and advanced, not allowing that poor choice to defeat her.

### Acknowledge

The more quickly we face our mistakes, the more quickly we can start acting on getting out of the circumstance. Abigail's approach to David shows us she readily accepted the fact that she was married to a fool and because of her connection to him, she was now in an awkward spot.

When Abigail saw David, she quickly got off her donkey and bowed down before David with her face to the ground. She fell at his feet and said: "My lord, let the blame be on me alone. Please let your servant speak to you; hear what your servant has to say. May my lord pay no attention to that wicked man Nabal. He is just like his name—his name is Fool, and folly goes with him. But as for me, your servant, I did not see the men my master sent" *(1 Sam. 25:23-25).*

Let go of your pride and acknowledge that you've made a mistake. It takes both courage and maturity to own up to your own accountability. So what if everyone will now know you aren't perfect? News flash. Everyone knows that already. You are really just making things worse if you continue down a path that is destructive. Don't be surprised either when the people from whom you're trying to hide this thing know your level of blame and involvement anyway.

I've been in Location 3 more times than I'd like to admit

and in more circumstances than I'm willing to share. But to make my point, I feel it necessary to give you a personal example.

I had been driving a Dodge Caravan for about four years. The note was paid and it was shuttling my little sons and me all over town just fine. However, it had started looking pretty ragged. For some reason, the paint had begun to chip off and large sections of the exterior looked like they had been scraped with steel wool pads. I wanted something newer and sleeker.

One day, I ventured onto a car lot "just to look" and, disregarding the fact that the last thing I needed was a car payment, I drove off the lot in a preowned yet newer-than-my-van cute little navy blue Jeep Cherokee. The fifth of each month started rolling around more and more quickly as did the payment date for the increased car insurance. I now couldn't afford regular maintenance at the dealership, and soon my Jeep was experiencing mechanical problems. I finally had to admit to myself and my husband that I had contributed to our financial struggle.

Acknowledging my poor choices in buying that Jeep didn't change my financial picture; it changed me. The admission humbled me and freed me to redirect my thinking. Instead of wasting time making excuses, I could now use that mental energy figuring out how to budget my way out of the fiduciary mess I was in.

Even if you think no one else is affected, at least acknowledge to yourself that you are suffering consequences in Location 3 because of a poor choice you made. Own your blame.

What are you currently suffering through because of a poor choice *you* made?

## Act Wisely

Now that you have been honest with yourself, you can transfer the energy you previously used to deflect blame and channel that power toward effecting positive change.

Abigail took the bull by the horns and approached David without Nabal's knowledge. "When Abigail went to Nabal, he was in the house holding a banquet like that of a king. He was in high spirits and very drunk. So she told him nothing until daybreak" (1 Sam. 25:36). She approached David with wise counsel, suggesting a solution that was best for him, regardless of how foolishly Nabal had acted.

To bring about positive change in her situation, Abigail had to act wisely in dealing with the man who was about to kill her husband. She appealed to David's knowledge of His divinely appointed future. In essence, she told him it wouldn't be good for the future king to have a track record of depending upon himself and not upon the Lord to fight his battles. She helped David focus on the larger picture. (Read 1 Sam. 25:28-31 if you're interested in her specific suggestion.)

What can you do to bring about positive change? In my case with the Jeep, I had to reallocate funds and impose a stricter budget on myself. I also had to redirect my thinking. I could not afford *not* to keep up regular maintenance if I expected to drive back and forth to my job—my main source of income.

It's impossible for me to give you every specific answer to your particular problem, but here are a few general guidelines that may be helpful:

*Finances:* If your poor choice has been in the area of finance, you probably have less discretionary money than you had before. The bottom line is that you form the mind-set and habit of living within your means. Pay your tithes first and modestly take care of the essentials: living quarters, transportation, food, and clothing. There are ways to cut back on these essentials even though you cannot cut them out completely.

- I saved $350 a month by buying a house. I moved from a $1,200-per-month apartment into a house in a middle-income area with an $850-per-month mortgage. Try to hold on to property you own, but in some cases, moving to less expensive digs may be necessary. If you own and have the room, take in a friend as a boarder for a while.

- You may need to drive more economically. I traded the Jeep and entered a lease on a new Toyota Camry, saving myself increasing repair costs.

- Severely curtail eating out. For the price of one dinner in a restaurant, you can buy groceries for a week. Eat breakfast and carry inexpensive snacks, like fruit, veggie sticks, or energy bars, for when you get hungry between meals.

- Live within a budget.

*Relationships:* If your poor choice involves a relationship, govern your actions regarding the other person according to what Scripture tells you.

Ladies, when dealing with men, first of all, any illicit relationships have to go. Adultery clearly violates Scripture. One of the Ten Commandments says, "Thou shalt not commit adultery" (Exod. 20:14, KJV). Pretty clear, right? No matter how good the man makes you feel, if either of you is married to someone else, end the relationship immediately.

If you're dealing with a man who is cheating on his wife, you are dealing with a man who is a cheat. Call a spade a spade. If you're the married one, then you're the cheat. Cheaters are not marriage material.

A sinful relationship is as addictive as alcohol or drugs. For the same reason you wouldn't put alcohol near the hands of an alcoholic, you don't put the temptation of an illicit relationship near a cheater. Remove yourself from relationships that could turn adulterous. The alcoholic or the drug addict must take drastic steps to change his or her lifestyle, mind-set, and habits. So must the adulterer. Also, do not commit sexual immorality. Again, Scripture is clear. "Flee from sexual immorality. All other sins a man commits are outside his body, but he who sins sexually sins against his own body" (1 Cor. 6:18).

One of my former students experienced a date rape. The trauma caused her self-esteem to plummet, and she compensated by becoming promiscuous. However, each act of fornication just served to erode her feelings about herself even more.

Your relationship problem might not be a sexual issue but could still involve your husband or serious boyfriend. For starters, married ladies, read Eph. 5:21-33, Titus 2:3-5, 1 Pet. 3:1-6, and Prov. 31 for biblical wisdom about being a wife.

Single ladies, you can use many of the same principles, except those passages dealing with sex, when relating with a serious boyfriend. However, if you are sensing for some reason that you made a poor choice in hooking up with this man, break up and go your own way. If you marry him without clearing up the problem, you'll find to your horror and dismay that living in a bad marriage is much worse than getting over a disappointing breakup.

If you've made poor choices in other types of relationships, one piece of general advice is found in Rom. 12:18. It says, "If it is possible, as far as it depends on you, live at peace with everyone."

What relationship needs your attention because it has been affected by or is a result of a poor choice?

Pray and search Scripture in regard to what your wise action should now be.

What is God directing you to do?

What is your confirmation?

*Employment:* What if your poor choice involves your employment? Good jobs are hard to come by. I know a woman whose husband began to feel he had chosen the wrong career. He had worked at his job for more than 15 years, had been promoted several times, and was receiving a comfortable salary that met his growing family's needs. So what did he do? He removed himself from his uncomfortable circumstance. True, quitting removed him from the consequences of his poor workplace choice, but it also removed him from the bank line.

Poor choices in your work environment may mean you need to come clean by admitting mistakes. Ask God how He would have you handle this.

What poor choice have you made regarding your employment?

What scriptural guidelines will you follow regarding how you should handle the situation you've caused?

*Advance and Move Forward:* Abigail made a poor choice in Nabal, her foolish husband, and she was living with the consequences of that choice. We have seen though that she acknowledged her poor choice and acted wisely despite it. After that, the natural result was that she moved forward with her life.

In spite of making a poor choice and suffering behind it, you can get past it and rise above it. Look at Phil. 3:13-14 (KJV): "Brethren, I count not myself to have apprehended: but this one thing I do, forgetting those things which are behind, and reaching forth unto those things which are before, I press toward the mark for the prize of the high calling of God in Christ Jesus." Once you are doing your best, it is God's loving nature to pour His best back out on you.

Look at the depiction of the father in the story of the prodigal son. (See Luke 15:11-32.) After this young man made horrible choices and ended up suffering in a pigpen because of them (a definite Location 3 consequence), he acknowledged his wrong and made the wise choice to return home. What happened next is illustrative of the advancement step.

*Expect Nothing:* First, he expected nothing. This prodigal young man had his speech all practiced. He thought it up while slopping around with the pigs and launched right into it as soon as he was reunited with his dad. "Father, I have sinned against heaven, and before thee, and am no more worthy to be called thy son: make me as one of thy hired servants" (Luke 15:18-19, KJV).

Once you've acknowledged your mistake and acted wisely toward rectifying it, you've done all you can do. You are not responsible for and cannot control anyone else's reactions. Expect nothing. That's probably the scariest part of 'fessing up. You don't know what the other person will do. Sometimes it goes well; sometimes it doesn't.

Some years ago, I blew it with my friend Linda. She had flown cross-country at her expense to be in my wedding. Two years later, she sent me her wedding invitation. I was pregnant with my first child and her wedding date was scheduled for just after my baby would be born. That date and a sudden pregnancy complication combined to make it impossible for me to attend her wedding.

Realizing I couldn't go, I planned to design and make a personalized gift—a satin pillow on which I would personally embroider the couple's names and the wedding date. I bought the fabric, lace trim, and thread. Then I birthed my baby.

New motherhood overwhelmed me. I was totally consumed with Matthew's care: nursing, changing, bathing, and so forth. Honestly, that satin pillow was far from my mind.

A month passed and I received a call from Linda. She was furious and hurt. She accused me of being thoughtless and selfish. All I could do was accept the rebuke and say I was sorry. I apologized again by mail, tried to explain what had happened, and asked for her forgiveness.

Unfortunately, Linda could not forgive me. Even after several years had passed and I was on vacation in her city, she did not want to talk to me when I called her.

I learned from my mistake and moved on. There was nothing more I could do, so I had to leave the issue in the past. I have tried to be a more thoughtful friend since then, even when I have lots on my plate (like I usually do). I've also learned the value, impact, and graciousness of granting forgiveness when it is asked of me.

*Accept Blessings:* Gratefully, more times than not, the reaction to your acknowledgment and action will be positive. So although you expect nothing, be ready to accept blessings.

For Abigail, her advancement came 10 days after she told her husband how she had saved his hide. The shock of facing his own folly caused his heart to fail. After he died, Abigail became the wife of David, the future king. Now that's advancement.

The prodigal's advancement happened immediately. His father readily forgave him, threw him a huge welcome home party, and reinstated his position in the family.

Regardless of the positive or negative response, God has a way of working everything out for good for those who love Him. Romans 8:28 says, "And we know that in all things God works for the good of those who love him, who have been called according to his purpose."

## Location 4: A Place You Did Not Choose

The fourth location you may find yourself in is one you did not choose. You are operating in Location 4 if your issues were thrust upon you by someone else. For example, you may have been born into your less-than-perfect circumstances. Maybe the actions of your husband or children have you in a difficult place. Or maybe your company or boss has thrust your life into mayhem.

You did not choose this location, and you can't change it. The question to ask is, "God, what do You expect of me right here, right now?" You want God to use you, so here's your opportunity to let Him.

Location 4 is exactly where the Israelites were in their

Egyptian bondage. They had done nothing wrong. They were just minding their own business in Egypt's best land—the land of Goshen—when a Pharaoh rose to power who had no affinity with their ancestors and no reason to believe their large population wouldn't conspire against him. To keep that from happening, he decided to enslave them. (See Exod. 1:8-11.)

The Israelites had no other choice but to live as slaves. They endured 430 years of harsh treatment, but in the end were released in a way that proved to Pharaoh—a man who thought he was a god—who God really was.

Other Bible stories illustrate that God sometimes allows us to live through difficult circumstances not of our choosing for a higher purpose.

- Esther entered a beauty contest and figured she might get a good husband out of the deal. She was indeed chosen and became the queen, but that put her in the tough situation to step up as the spokesperson for her race, to save them from a holocaust. (See the Book of Esther.)

- Job was an entrepreneur who had raised a large family and built a successful business. God and Satan discussed Job's spirituality, which Satan challenged. In essence, God told Satan to do his worst to see if Job would cave, just don't kill him. Job had no idea why his whole life suddenly collapsed all around him. God's belief in this one man was on the line. If Job had failed, Satan would have proven that people only serve God for what He does for them and God would have looked pretty bad.

The morning I was finishing this part of this chapter, one of the assistant pastors at my church preached a message titled "A Lesson from the Cross-bearer." Mark 15:21 tells of

Simon the Cyrenian, a visitor to Jerusalem on the day of Jesus' crucifixion, who was caught in an experience he did not plan. Scripture tells us he was compelled, forced by the Roman soldiers, to carry Jesus' cross for Him to Golgotha. It wasn't Simon's cross and carrying it wasn't Simon's choice, but the experience made him persevere and brought him closer to Christ. One of Simon's children is even mentioned in Rom. 16:13 as one serving Christ himself.

If you are in Location 4, remember that whatever the catalyst that put you where you are, God is in control. God was in control when Esther, Job, and Simon faced their situations, and since they let God do what He wanted to do, they grew closer to Him and He ultimately received glory.

See your difficulty as a chance for God to shine. First Corinthians 10:31 says, "Whether therefore ye eat, or drink, or whatsoever ye do, do all to the glory of God" (KJV). God doesn't do the impossible until all your possibilities prove impossible. If it takes suffering to accomplish what God would have us do, Peter says we should rejoice to be used in this way. "But rejoice that you participate in the sufferings of Christ, so that you may be overjoyed when his glory is revealed" (1 Pet. 4:13).

Identify situations you are facing that no actions of your own have caused.


Surrender to God's sovereignty. Write a prayer here to that effect.

This is the whole point—bring God glory. Indeed, this point could be seen as a conclusion for the other three locations as well. In Location 1, when all is well in your life, use the time to grow closer to the Lord and encourage others thereby bringing God glory. In Location 2, when you've chosen well but are experiencing unexpected outcomes, don't worry, just stand in truth. These reactions will bring God glory. In Location 3, when you are where you are due to poor choices, God receives glory when you acknowledge your mistake, act wisely, and advance by looking forward. If you are in Location 4, remember that God is in control and your difficulty is a chance for God to shine.

## ♠ Four
# Inclination
## What Do I Accept as Truth?

### Sniffing Out the Onions

Whether you had a hand in planning your current location or not, now that you have an understanding of that location, your next step is to be aware of your place in God's plan, in His scheme of things. Never lose sight of the fact that we are strangers and pilgrims on the earth. (See 1 Pet. 2:11.) We're just passing through. A contemporary Christian song says that we are strangers, we are aliens; we are not of this world.

Remaining aware of and alert to who we are in Christ is vital to keeping us on the right track spiritually and ultimately experientially. If we become too comfortable in any situation, we risk losing sight of what God intends for us.

Remaining alert means we'll be able to detect the smell and taste of leeks and onions in "dishes" that could be disguised as milk and honey. Do you want that job only because of the money (a leeks/onions reason) or because God is placing you in a new position (a milk/honey reason)? Are you after that man only because he looks good and has resources that can pull you out of debt (a leeks/onions reason), or are you drawn to him because you can be his helpmate for the rest of his life (a milk/honey reason)?

As children of God, there should always be a God-inspired reason why we are involved in any circumstance. And wherever we are, God can be glorified through our lives in that place if we allow Him to touch the situation through us. However, if we're not careful, we can become comfortable with the wrong things.

This is what happened to the Israelites. Once they got to Egypt, the land of Goshen got very comfortable for them. They were initially moved there to escape famine. Once the famine passed, things were so good in Goshen that they stayed. As I mentioned in chapter 1, it could be that God allowed them to stay for the express purpose of taking them through the Egyptian captivity. Whether this theory is factual or not, the point is the same. We must always seek God's mind and heart in relation to what He would have us do in our particular situation.

Memorize Phil. 4:6-7: "Do not be anxious about anything, but in everything, by prayer and petition, with thanksgiving, present your requests to God. And the peace of God, which transcends all understanding, will guard your hearts and your minds in Christ Jesus."

1. Ask God to help you understand your situation. As you begin to sniff out leeks-and-onions issues possibly disguised as milk-and-honey issues, define them.

2. Ask God to show you how to eliminate the leeks and onions and develop a taste for milk-and-honey replacements.

Psalm 1:1 says, "Blessed is the man that walketh not in the counsel of the ungodly, nor standeth in the way of sinners, nor sitteth in the seat of the scornful" (KJV). Walking in the counsel of the ungodly, standing in the way of sinners, and sitting in the seat of the scornful are the three progressive steps that slide us Christians downward, causing us to be less and less sensitive to detecting leeks and onions.

When we are clicking on all cylinders with God, we easily sniff out the smell of onionlike issues. We immediately smell a rat in the guy who approaches us with a slick one-liner. We say no to the mixed drink at the party that is making everybody else so fabulously friendly. It's even easy to turn off an overly racy movie. That guy, the drink, and the movie? All onions. We smelled them right away because through regular prayer times and consistent Bible reading, we are consciously keeping ourselves in tune with the Lord.

However, we can allow ourselves to listen less and less to the voice of the Holy Spirit. Psalm 1 warns us of the slippery slope we can slide down if we are not vigilantly keeping a sharp eye out and our noses calibrated for detecting leeks and onions.

First, walking in the counsel of the ungodly has to do with initial exposure to ideas that are not of God. You stop to look at the leeks and onions growing in the garden of your circumstances. At this stage of the game, you just look and listen, becoming aware of what another person thinks. The only problem is that this other person is not talking about things that would build you up and make you a better Christian. To the contrary, the ideas you are hearing don't take God into account. They may not be blatantly against God on the surface, but they certainly are not ideas that point to Him either.

For example, the idea of safe sex is ungodly counsel. People gain the belief that condoms protect them from pregnancy and all sexually transmitted diseases. Well, condoms may protect to some degree against unwanted pregnancy and against some diseases, but they do not take care of the bigger problem of sexual promiscuity. God says to save sex for marriage. Any sexual intercourse outside of marriage places you in peril with God because you are in sin. Being in peril with God certainly is not safe.

The counsel of the ungodly is insidious because it comes

on the lips of those we have come to trust. This counsel can come through friends or family members we've known for years, authors of books or columns we've always read and enjoyed, and the visual media via television (including the news) and movies.

My son Matthew gave me a great example of this point. Our family viewed *Ray*, the critically acclaimed movie that earned an academy award for Jamie Foxx for his incredible portrayal of the performer's life. Foxx literally seemed to become Ray Charles on the screen. After our viewing, I asked Matthew how he liked the movie. Amid all the praise everyone else was heaping on the film, Matthew shrugged and commented, "Ray Charles was a drug addict and an adulterer."

Matthew had not been so blinded by the incredible acting and the well-told biography of this famous personality that he missed the serious flaws in Charles's character. Despite Ray Charles's obvious musical genius and business savvy, his glaring moral failures eliminated him from Matthew's list of people he wants to emulate.

All too often, young people are not able to draw that line, and they allow a person's celebrity to excuse their detrimental shortcomings. Way too many people, both young and old, not only excuse the negatives but also justify and imitate them because those people involved are in the limelight. When we start entertaining wrong values, giving them a possibility of acceptance just by our consideration, we are walking in the counsel of the ungodly. We start to become just a little less sensitive to the scent of onions.

Not only does Ps. 1 warn us against walking in the counsel of the ungodly, but it also warns us against standing in the way of sinners. Now this doesn't mean we are in a sinner's way, somehow obstructing his progress. Standing in the way of sinners means we are now becoming comfortable with those ungodly ideas we have been hearing. We are harvesting the leeks and onions, handling them, and admiring how they look and smell. We begin to agree with ungodly ideas by considering what's being said and even beginning to take that side of the argument when the issue arises.

The sinner referred to in this scripture is physically involved in the action of the ungodly idea, and we are comfortable with this person and his or her lifestyle. Although we are not yet involved in the commission of the sin, we argue his or her right to feel and think the way he or she does, not taking into consideration that his or her feelings and thoughts are sinful in God's eyes.

In our safe sex example, we now defend the rights of teens to receive condoms at school and get abortions without parental notification or permission. When we keep our mouths shut about the wrongs of premarital sex and abortion we find ourselves in the walking-in-the-counsel category.

In our *Ray* example, our standing-in-the-way answer to Matthew's pointed revelation is, "Everybody has little imperfections, but Charles's genius far overshadowed them, thus making him a good role model. You shouldn't talk about the negatives in a person."

That sounds hypocritical to me. At no other time and in no other area do we allow the model to be substantively different from the real thing. If the model or prototype is not almost exactly the same, it's not considered a model, but something different. With role models, the standard should be the same. Everything about the role model, if copied, ought to reflect the respectable, moral, decent human being you are trying to be like. If substantive areas of that person's life don't measure up to the standard you would be proud to live by, then that person should not be a role model for you.

1. List the names of your role models. (Be honest.)


2. What is it about each person you listed that would make him or her a prime candidate for being your role model?


3. What is it about each person you listed that would eliminate him or her from being your role model?


4. Taking your answers to numbers 2 and 3 above, are the people on your list still good role models?


Third, sitting in the seat of the scornful finds us going past mental assent to participation. We are now ingesting leeks and onions, happily cooking with them, and serving them up as our specialty.

At least the ungodly person and the sinner allowed God's view to be one of the many views in consideration. It's just that God's views were not the view of choice. By contrast, the scornful person blatantly says that God is wrong and his or her idea (which is clearly opposite of God's Word) is right. When we reach the point where we are sitting in the seat of the scornful, we are comfortable in their seat, taking part in their sin. Need we complete what this means in our safe sex example?

I've seen an example of this slide in the life of a married girlfriend who began to consider the possibility that she could be a lesbian. In her case, she walked in the counsel of the ungodly throughout much of her childhood. She was exposed to influences that her impressionable mind took in and processed on its own, without the benefit of Christian insight to properly explain the perversions she was seeing and, in some cases, being encouraged to participate in.

As an adult, this friend of mine allowed herself to be surrounded by people who found no real fault with the homosexual lifestyle. As a matter of fact, there were homosexual people she met who treated her better than some straight Christians had treated her. She began to stand with those "sinners," mentally agreeing with their warped philosophy about relationships. Once in the standing mode, sitting in the seat of the scornful was a very short move. Once she became convinced of what they were saying, she began to conform her actions to their lifestyle.

That friend and her husband divorced, breaking apart their family, which included four children. She "married" her lesbian partner and began raising her children as part of her homosexual relationship.

Fortunately, the last time I talked with her about all of this, her spirit was still uncomfortable to some extent. She had spent years in a solid, Bible-teaching ministry, and I believe the Holy Spirit can still communicate with her heart. Pray for my friend.

## Stopping the Slide

Yes, it's only too easy to accelerate quickly from walking in the counsel of the ungodly, through standing in the way of sinners, to sitting in the seat of the scornful. The seat of the scornful is a leeks-and-onions position. The only way to put the brakes on a slide down this slippery slope is to make some immediate, deliberate changes. The further down the slope you are, the more radical the change has to be.

For example, at the walking-in-the-counsel stage, when my friend first became aware of her thoughts about homosexuality, she could have dedicated herself to prolonged prayer and sought Christian counseling. The Word of God could have been a source of strength as she searched the Scriptures to find God's heart and mind on the subject of homosexuality and then determine to live by His design.

If she didn't recognize her problem until the standing-in-the-way stage, in addition to prayer, counseling, and Bible study, my friend should have separated herself from those who held ideas different from God's Word on the subject. This, of course, would have been harder to do because once friendships have been established, separations are painful. It hurts to lose your friend, and it hurts to hurt others' feelings. She would have risked looking like a hypocrite to her friends because, up until that point, she had not been challenging anything they believed.

Then, if the realization didn't come until the sitting-in-the-seat stage, she would have to take drastic steps. She'd need prayer, counseling, Bible study, separation, and extensive work with organizations specializing in ministering to people who have been deceived by the homosexual lifestyle. She would need to confess to those immediately involved in her life. She would have to patiently and consistently work to prove her true willingness to change her lifestyle.

Our present-day society makes it easy for us to be comfortable with issues completely contrary to God and His Word. As Christians, we should not hold personal opinions that are contrary to the Word of God. What we think, feel, and espouse ought to line up with what God thinks, feels, and espouses. If we are allowing ourselves to believe things that are contrary to what God's Word teaches, we are operating in disobedience, not allowing God to conform us into the image of His Son. (See Rom. 8:29.)

Consider the following issues. In light of our current discussion about our inclinations and what we accept as truth, evaluate your position. Pay attention to your initial reactions. They are usually true of how you really feel. If your views contradict God's, sniff out the onions. Start immediately to change your views to agree with how God sees things. Pay attention to your thoughts, words, and actions in your personal problem areas.

## Racism

My kids helped me notice that I can make racist statements every now and then. For example, when watching television shows about family life, my boys have heard me comment about the differences between how white TV families and Black TV families discipline their children. The white kids on TV are allowed to talk back to their parents and the parents allow it, sometimes even complimenting the children on how astute their observations have been. By contrast, remembering back to *The Cosby Show,* the African-American Huxtable children got into serious trouble whenever they tried to smart-talk their parents. I used this distinction in an effort to point out to my boys that disrespectful talk and attitudes are not tolerated in our house.

Well, the next time a real-life disciplining situation came up in our conversation, I heard my boys make the same racial distinction that I had made. They had taken my comments to mean that Black parents were better at disciplining their children than white parents. I wanted them to understand they couldn't get away with talking back to me, but I had used race to make my point, thereby stereotyping all white families.

Stereotyping by race is a racist thing to do, and it's not right. I had to correct the faulty impression I had left with my children. I believe it is true that TV kids speak very disrespectfully to their parents. However, I should not have tied that observation to race. Besides, much that is broadcast on television is stereotypical and untrue about Black people, and I certainly don't want white people getting the idea that I'm anything like the majority of what the media puts out there about my race.

Be careful of the comments you make in front of your children, coworkers, and acquaintances that might be misconstrued as racially demeaning. The Golden Rule can definitely be applied here (Matt. 7:12) as can Gal. 5:14, which tells us to love our neighbor as we love ourselves. The word *neighbor* comes from a word meaning "fellowman" and that crosses racial lines.

## Abortion

I've taught in Christian schools for 15 years and have talked with quite a few teenagers who found themselves confronted with an unplanned pregnancy. It is always interesting when I help the student approach his or her parents. Several times, I have been shocked to find the initial reaction of these Christian parents was to suggest abortion.

What is your position on abortion? Is it the same as God's? Do you know the facts? Will your position on abortion change if an unplanned pregnancy occurs in your family? God's truth does not change because of the situation; neither should our truths change based on situational ethics.

Be it the life of the preborn infant or the life of the severely handicapped, God holds life valuable. He went on to validate the importance of the life of the preborn child in Exod. 21:22-23, which says, "If men who are fighting hit a pregnant woman and she gives birth prematurely but there is no serious injury, the offender must be fined whatever the woman's husband demands and the court allows. But if there is serious injury, you are to take life for life."

## Homosexuality

God's position on homosexuality is clear. He responds quite negatively to the practice. In Gen. 19, God destroyed a whole city—wiped it clean off the map—because of the sin of homosexuality. God's Word is also clear in Lev. 18:22, "Do not lie with a man as one lies with a woman; that is detestable," and 20:13, "If a man lies with a man as one lies with a woman, both of them have done what is detestable. They must be put to death; their blood will be on their own heads."

The Old Testament is not the only place that mentions homosexuality as a sin. Read Rom. 1:24-27. In this passage, God allows people who want to persist in this sin to receive the punishment inherent in that kind of lifestyle. It's like God is saying, "Go on then. I tried to warn you, now you'll be sorry." First Corinthians 6:9-10 makes the point as clearly as can be said: "Do you not know that the wicked will not inherit the kingdom of God? Do not be deceived: Neither the sexually immoral nor idolaters nor adulterers nor male prostitutes nor homosexual offenders, nor thieves nor the greedy nor drunkards nor slanderers nor swindlers will inherit the kingdom of God."

Can you square your views and reactions on the subject with God's views and reactions? How do you respond to the politically correct idea of tolerance? What's the difference between tolerance and acceptance?

As Christians, however uncomfortable others try to make us, we are obligated to feel about issues the way God feels about those same issues. Yet, we are still called upon to respond in every situation out of a heart of love and compassion. We are to be like Christ on both ends of the spectrum —hate the sin; love the sinner. Speak the truth in love (Eph. 4:15).

## Divorce

"But he won't work."

"We just can't get along."

"We're going different directions in life."

"I'm sick of his inattention."

"When we got married, I thought I could get him to become a Christian, but after all these years, he still hasn't accepted Christ."

"He doesn't understand me."

"This marriage isn't turning out like I thought it would."

California and many other states in the United States have what's called no-fault divorce. Any of the above excuses is good enough to end your marriage. But no matter what the law says, none of the above excuses is a biblical excuse for leaving your marriage.

What does God say about marriage? What does He really mean by *submission?* What is God's intention for marriage? Are your ideas lined up with God's on the subject of divorce?

Malachi 2:16 reads, "'I hate divorce,' says the LORD God of Israel." God intended for marriages to last until the death of a spouse. Why? First, God made man and woman for each other, to complement and to help each other. Marriage and family are God's ideas. (See Gen. 2:18-24.)

Second, the married couple is a picture to the world of the union between Christ and the Church. Ephesians 5:18-33, the great passage on marriage, ends with Paul tying the two together. What we thought was just an earthly relationship really is a spiritual reflection. The husband's love and sacrifice for his wife is the picture of Christ's love and sacrifice for us. The wife's submission and honor for her husband is a picture of our submission and honor for Christ. When we divorce, we sully the picture.

God has given us two exceptions, situations in which He will allow divorce, but the reasons stemmed from our hard hearts. One exception is if there has been infidelity (Matt. 19:9) and the other is desertion (1 Cor. 7:10-15).

I have also heard it suggested that physical abuse falls under the category of desertion because abuse disregards the vows of love and commitment promised. The abuser has already deserted his or her vows. Also, by staying in the marriage, the abused mate is allowing his or her body, which is God's temple, to be defiled.

If you are in an abusive relationship, you must remove yourself for the sake of your physical safety. Then, before filing for divorce, pray much, seek God's wisdom for your marriage, and listen to the godly counsel of Christian witnesses like your pastor or a Christian marriage, family, and child therapist. Prov. 15:22 instructs, "Without counsel, plans go awry, but in the multitude of counselors they are established" (NKJV).

## Movies

What movies do you like to watch? Are they edifying? What underlying message about God, Christians, and morality is being taught in the movie? Are you recommending movies to others that undermine what you believe as a child of God?

Scrutinize your entertainment in light of the Word of God. Again, sniff out the onions. Why do you like what you like? Would you be comfortable watching that particular movie with Jesus sitting next to you? I don't think Jesus is a prude, and I think He has a sense of humor; I'm just challenging you to think about your whole life as the witness for Christ that it is.

My husband and I were recently watching a comedian on a cable television special. He was joking about married couples and much of what he said was pretty funny because it was so right on. He then launched into a sequence about Adam and Eve's first sexual encounter. I laughed at first as he portrayed Adam's wide-eyed ecstasy at seeing Eve for the first time, especially after he had just named all the animals only to find no suitable companion. Although I watched the whole sketch, I felt uncomfortable. It was just something about using the Bible characters in that way that seemed wrong. Yes, I'm the first person to espouse that Bible characters were ordinary people just like us, but his jokes made their first sexual encounter lewd rather than beautiful and holy, as sex was truly meant to be.

## Toys

A toy fad once caused me a personal problem. It was the fad of the little electronic pets. I felt that students had to spend a disproportionate amount of time with the toy. The pet's care required that it be carried by the student constantly. Teens could be seen wearing them on key chains, around their necks, and on their belts. When schools started banning the toys because students were more concerned with their electronic baby than with their schoolwork, some parents got into the act and took their child's "pet" to work to keep it alive.

I didn't see these children lavishing that much attention on or spending even a fraction of that time with the Word of God. Because of my observations, my children were not allowed to own the electronic pets, and I helped them understand why.

What types of toys do you allow your kids to play with? Have you ever thought to compare the amount of time your child spends playing video games with the amount of time he or she spends on spiritual pursuits like reading the Bible or memorizing Scripture? Perhaps you're not too hard on your children concerning how they spend their free time because you are playing with your own toys for a disproportionate amount of time yourself. How much time do you waste on e-mail or the phone? Is the work you bring home from the office swallowing up your personal Bible study and prayer time?

Racism, abortion, homosexuality, divorce, movies, and toys: these are just a handful of issues we face. What do you accept as truth about the music you like to listen to, drinking alcoholic beverages, and assisted suicide? Have you developed a taste for leeks and onions in these or any other areas? I challenge you to sniff out leeks and onions in your own outlooks, attitudes, and opinions.

Are there situations in your life that should make you more uncomfortable than they do?

Evaluate what stage you're in and take the necessary steps to get off the slippery slope.

Are you walking in the counsel of the ungodly?

1. What advice are you listening to that's contrary to the Word of God?

2. Pray for God's deliverance.

3. Seek Christian counsel about your current situation or belief.

Are you standing in the way of sinners?

1. What do you agree with that the Bible is clearly against?


2. Pray for God's deliverance.

3. Seek Christian counsel about your current situation or belief.

4. Separate yourself from the people who are influencing you by the beliefs they hold that contradict God's Word.


Are you sitting in the seat of the scornful?

1. What are you actively involved in that is clearly against Scripture?


2. Pray for God's deliverance.

3. Seek Christian counsel about your current situation or belief.

4. Separate yourself from the people who are influencing you by the beliefs they hold that contradict God's Word.

5. Make yourself accountable to your immediate family, your pastor, and a mature Christian counselor of your same gender who can disciple you regularly.

# Five

# Evaluation

## What Do I Lack from My Past?

There was a very popular television drama series back in the '80s called *Dallas*. It told the story of the Ewing family, rich cattlemen who got into all kinds of messes. Known for its season-ending cliff-hangers, the show left the viewing audience talking all summer about what might possibly happen next year.

One season ended unbelievably. Bobby, the younger, morally conscious, likeable brother, died. We faithful watchers agonized through the entire next season with Pam, his understandably devastated wife, as she floundered through each episode, grieving, struggling with the antics of her wicked in-laws, and trying to make sense of life without Bobby.

As that season came to a close, we sat transfixed watching the cliff-hanger, wondering how Pam would ever make it. Then suddenly, she arose from a fitful nap hearing water running in her bathroom. She could see through the beveled enclosure that someone was in there. She opened the door to find—to her shock and ours—Bobby happily washing his hair in the shower!

The entire season had been nothing but a bad dream. I guess the writers didn't know how they were going to get their characters out of all the jams they had gotten them into all year, so they just wiped the slate totally clean and started over.

If you're normal, unless you are a person in Location 1 where all is well, you've probably wanted at times to wake up and find it's all been a bad dream. *Why can't I wake out of this*

*nightmare?* you ask. Unfortunately, our present discomforts and our pasts are not dreams; they are realities, and we have to face them.

The Israelites lived 430 years in the nightmare of their bondage in Egypt, and as hard as it is to believe, that was part of God's plan for them. Like us, they had to face their dilemma and deal with it the best they could, hoping in God for their escape. Unbeknownst to them, God was toughening them up, giving them something impossible to get out of on their own. He fixed it so they had no other choice but to look to Him for deliverance.

And just as God knows us, He knew His people the Israelites. Look at their track record once they actually did get into the Promised Land. At every opportunity, they had a habit of getting sucked up, completely immersed, into whatever culture surrounded them. They would worship the gods of those people and follow their rituals rather than staying true to God. Perhaps their Egyptian bondage was the method God used at that time to assure that they would remain distinct. With their tendency, if they hadn't been in bondage to the Egyptians, they may have taken on all the Egyptian traits and habits and never left Egypt at all. The bondage was necessary to move them forward.

Does God get more of your concentrated attention when all is well with you or when you're experiencing difficulties?

Throughout the Bible, we read of God's tendency to operate through and in spite of the negative circumstances His people encountered in their pasts. As devastating as the problem may have been, God not only fixed it but added a positive surprise consequence for good measure. Look at the situation that brought the Israelites to Egypt in the first place.

Joseph's brothers sold him to folks who took him to

Egypt and sold him again (see Gen. 37:28)—a definite negative experience. However, through a series of amazing events, Joseph ended up being vice-Pharaoh and had the authority to move his entire family into the land of Goshen, the best land in Egypt, saving them from starvation because of the famine. Joseph's brothers meant for their act to destroy him, but God knew that their treachery and Joseph's subsequent trials were necessary to get him where God wanted him to be. When Joseph finally stands face-to-face with the now-fearful brothers who had betrayed him, he articulates the conclusion of his understanding of his past: "When Joseph's brothers saw that their father was dead, they said, 'What if Joseph holds a grudge against us and pays us back for all the wrongs we did to him?'" Joseph responded, "You intended to harm me, but God intended it for good to accomplish what is now being done, the saving of many lives" (Gen. 50:15, 20).

Joseph's brothers sold him into slavery. God's fix was getting him out and making him vice-Pharaoh. The positive surprise consequence was reconciliation with his brothers and saving his entire family.

Consider these other examples of God's work in fixing a past problem and then adding a surprise:

Ruth lost her husband but gained another, and that new union placed her in the family line that led to the Messiah. (See the Book of Ruth.)

In 2 Sam. 4:4 and 9:6-10, we read about Mephibosheth, the lame son of Jonathan, King David's best friend. His handicap made it necessary for someone else to hide him. That hiding saved his life, and once his identity and his plight were discovered by David, he was allowed to eat daily at the king's table.

Paul's thorn in the flesh kept him humble before God,

and we have much of the New Testament thanks to Paul's submissive spirit before the Lord.

Of course, our utmost example of God turning a negative into a positive and adding a surprise twist was when He himself came to us in the person of Jesus Christ and died for our sins. Hallelujah for the surprise of the Resurrection that now makes salvation possible for us.

So you see, God has established a pattern of taking our past jams and turning them into present jewels. God hasn't changed. He regularly takes what we initially understand as evil and flips the script on us, working things out to our advantage. He can do the same when we're dealing with negative issues from our past that affect our present. If we would just learn to hold out, stay strong, and trust God in the hard times, we would see the fabulous surprises God has in store for us on the other side of our problems.

## Looking Back

Lines from an old hymn say, "It is no secret what God can do. / What He's done for others, He'll do for you." God can make sense out of your past. He can redeem the difficult problems you have faced just like He did for the people in the Bible. Although it may be uncomfortable, it will be helpful to take a look back and do some self-evaluation of our pasts to see if what happened to us then could possibly have any bearing on what is happening to us now. Since we are a collection of what we received or did not receive from our family of origin, a look back may bring insight into why we have made the decisions we've made in the past, why we are making the decisions we make in the present, and why we are in our current location.

In their book *The Gift of the Blessing,* Drs. Gary Smalley and John Trent discuss how the Bible lays out the necessity for the family blessing. Based upon a study of various Old Testament passages, they show that a family should pass along this five-point blessing to their children, allowing them to grow into balanced individuals. Their definition of the blessing is as follows: "A family blessing begins with *meaningful touching*. It continues with a *spoken message* of *high value*, a message that pictures a *special future* for the individual being blessed, and one that is based on an *active commitment* to see the blessing come to pass." (Reprinted by permission of Thomas Nelson Inc., Nashville, TN., from the book entitled *The Gift of the Blessing*, copyright date 1993, by Gary Smalley and John Trent. All rights reserved.)

Drs. Trent and Smalley then go on to explain each element of the blessing. They talk about why each element is important and suggest how parents should pass each element along to their children. It's a great book that I highly recommend you read.[1]

As I read *The Gift of the Blessing*, I was evaluating my childhood to see if I had received these elements from my family. I was also determined to pass the blessing on to my own children. I began to wonder why everyone didn't receive these elements—they seem so natural. Then it occurred to me. Satan intends to thwart the passing of this blessing. Satan is against all things godly; therefore, Satan is against you, against me, and against our children receiving God's best, which would include God's blessing. For each element of the blessing that will enrich your life, Satan has a counterfeit that will ruin your life. Perhaps your present location and some of the issues you are facing are a result of the fact that Satan was able to counterfeit elements of the blessing in your life.

# Part 1: Evaluating Meaningful Touch

According to the definition above, "A family blessing begins with *meaningful touching.*" God began human life by touching Adam and Eve to create them. The seas brought forth the sea creatures and the earth brought forth the other living animals (Gen. 1:20, 24), but God formed Adam from the dust of the ground (2:7), molding him purposefully into the perfect form, and He built Eve from Adam's rib (v. 22), shaping her just right to be Adam's helpmate. (So, ladies, when someone compliments your figure by talking about your "build," that's biblically accurate!)

God began human life with His touch. Throughout Scripture, touch remains special. The laying on of hands symbolizes the impartation of the Spirit of God for particular service. For example, in Acts 6:6, when the apostles needed help, men were chosen for the task and hands were laid upon them. Also, in 1 Tim. 4:14, Paul instructs Timothy to remember his spiritual gift. He became aware of this gift when others prophesied and laid hands on him.

Touching is essential to healthy development. In college, I studied some psychologist who actually experimented with tactile deprivation. Children who were denied physical touch developed all sorts of psychological problems.

Touching is also an important way to express love. We hug and kiss people who are special to us. I remember hearing a news report some years ago on the calming effects of massaging babies and small children. Very few things feel as relaxing and as soothing as a great massage. No wonder spas are springing up all over town. Getting a massage is not just for the rich and famous anymore. The benefits of physical touch are the reason for the growth of this industry.

I loved holding my babies. I totally ignored all the warnings that said I would spoil them if I held them too much. My children grew up with a healthy balance of time playing with their toys, crawling around on their own, and being held in my arms, but I rarely denied them when they wanted to be held. Time moves much too fast, and sometimes now that they are in their upper teens, I long for those times when all they wanted to do was be held by their mama.

I also nursed my babies. What close, physical-touch times those were. The initial reciprocal effect was astounding. My babies were getting the nourishment they needed for life directly from my body, and I could feel the massaging and shrinking of my uterus as they suckled those first few weeks. We would look into each other's eyes as they nursed, and I could tell that an unbreakable bond was being formed through this close, physical touch.

I'll also never forget the tingle that flew up and down my spine the first time my husband gently drew me close, looked me in my eyes, and said, "I love you." The most intimate touches are shared by husband and wife and should always be beautiful moments. My most favorite place on earth is in my husband's arms.

Satan's perversion of meaningful touch is abuse. Touch was meant for blessing and healing, not for betrayal and hurt. Meaningful, physical touch calms and soothes; abuse causes fear. Since touch is so important and we crave it as essential to our development, we can get used to the wrong kind of touch. This is why physical abuse is so damaging. We accept abusive touch rather than settle for not being touched at all.

Abuse is most damaging when a person who is supposed to love us misuses physical touch. When parents, spouses, and children abuse each other physically, Satan robs us by perverting the blessing of touch.

Let me quickly say here that I am not against spanking your children. Proverbs clearly shares the wisdom of doing so. If you need some verses to support this, look at these few on the subject:

- "Do not withhold discipline from a child; if you punish him with the rod, he will not die. Punish him with the rod and save his soul from death" (Prov. 23:13-14).
- "He who spares the rod hates his son, but he who loves him is careful to discipline him" (13:24).
- "The rod of correction imparts wisdom, but a child left to himself disgraces his mother" (29:15).
- "Folly is bound up in the heart of a child, but the rod of discipline will drive it far from him" (22:15).

We slip into abuse when we hit children out of anger with a view only to punish instead of to discipline. When inappropriate smacking and hitting occurs from parent to child, we cannot pass the blessing of meaningful touch along.

Unfortunately, some children experience sexual abuse from close family members. Touch, which is supposed to re-assure, instead brings fear and hurt. It is especially heinous when the abuser is the child's father. This broken trust distorts a little girl's or a little boy's innocent love for Daddy, thus distorting the child's ability to love and trust a Heavenly Father. This is one of Satan's crowning achievements.

As an adult, I was physically abused in a relationship and it was devastating. It was confusing, embarrassing, and painful. I wondered, *How could this person be treating me this way?* I think I had the strength to deal with it immediately because I received the element of meaningful touch from my family. We weren't the real touchy-feely kind of folks, but there were hugs and kisses. I especially remember bedtime every night. I'd kiss Daddy good-night and he'd be sure to try to scratch my lips with the day's growth of stubble on his cheeks. It was a tender game that involved touch accompanied by the loving twinkle in his eyes.

So what if you did not receive meaningful touch as a

child? Reach out to Jesus now. Hebrews 4:15 says, "For we have not an high priest which cannot be touched with the feeling of our infirmities; but was in all points tempted like as we are, yet without sin" (KJV).

Jesus feels your pain. Through prayer you can do what His contemporaries did in person: you can touch Him and be made whole. Mark 6:56 says that wherever He went, "They begged him to let them touch even the edge of his cloak, and all who touched him were healed." Reach out to Jesus in prayer and allow Him to touch your heart and heal it.

Did you receive meaningful touch in your life as a child? If you did:

How was the element of meaningful touch passed to you?

How do you plan to pass it along to your children or loved ones?

If not:

How did Satan pervert meaningful touch in your life as a child?

Write a prayer asking for God's relief of this pain and restoration through His touch.

## Part 2: Evaluating Spoken Message

Family blessing also involves what we say. The blessing itself is verbalized; it is spoken aloud.

The Bible has some great things to say about positive words.

- "Pleasant words are a honeycomb, sweet to the soul and healing to the bones" (Prov. 16:24).

- "Reckless words pierce like a sword, but the tongue of the wise brings healing" (12:18).

- "The tongue that brings healing is a tree of life, but a deceitful tongue crushes the spirit" (15:4).

The Bible shows a relationship between the spoken words we hear and our physical health and spiritual well-being. That's pretty incredible. It makes sense to know that a spoken message is one of the elements of the family blessing and, as such, it's a target for satanic attack.

Jesus gives us the most amazing spoken message in His great invitation. In Matt. 11:28, He says, "Come to me, all you who are weary and burdened, and I will give you rest." What a positive message directed to anyone having a hard time. Is that you sometimes? (I know, some of you are saying, "That's me all the time!") Jesus' words are welcoming and inviting. They are words you want to fall into like a soft, newly-made bed covered with comfy throw pillows.

The world understands the importance of word messages. There's a multibillion-dollar business out there dedicated to attracting you with words. It's called advertising and marketing. Drive down any highway. Billboards are everywhere screaming at you with words telling you where you should bank, whom you should vote for, when you should go on vacation, why you should listen to a certain radio station, and what to eat, drive, buy, and watch on television. Once you get home and sift through junk mail full of more enticing words, you turn on the television only to be told every 8 to 12 minutes that you need the new car that's just in at the showroom down the street; you're thirsty for the new taste in soda; and your husband's sex drive can be reignited by the latest pill out on the market (but don't worry about those side effects—they hardly ever happen).

Since there are so many words being bandied about, it is more important than ever to be sure our children hear a positive spoken message from us. What they hear from people they admire most is what they will believe. If Mom and Dad say they are good for nothing, children will internalize that message and act like they are good for nothing. If children hear they are loved, they will act like people whom someone loves.

Evaluate the spoken messages you received as a little girl. Did you hear that you were good and smart? If so, you probably acted accordingly. Did you hear that you were ugly or worthless? If that was the case, you may have low self-esteem still today. Even if you could have handled it, you may have steered clear of running for cheerleader or for a class office because you felt bad about yourself thanks to negative words that had been spoken into your life.

Good words are necessary. They let us know we are genuinely accepted for who we are, not for what someone wants us to be.

Satan's perversion of the spoken message is accusation. One of Satan's identifying names is accuser of the brethren. (See Rev. 12:10.) He is trying to accuse us of our unworthiness before God, but Jesus is our Advocate with the Father God, ever defending us with His blood. And while we are supposed to be receiving positive spoken messages, Satan tries his best to make sure someone fills our ears with accusations.

This brand of perversion plays itself out in emotional abuse. I recently watched a popular daytime talk show that exposed husbands who constantly berated their wives. Those women had little or no self-esteem left. They stayed with their husbands because they genuinely loved them, but they were crying out for relief from the incessant badgering that had killed their joy.

Clarissa (not her real name) experienced emotional abuse in her first marriage and she didn't even know what was happening. Her husband used to tell her that she had problems because she did not live as the Christian she claimed to be. He conveniently left out the fact that he was seeing another woman and had stopped working to provide for Clarissa and their two young children. Especially toward the end of their marriage, when the abuse and neglect (and the abuse *of* neglect) got out of control, he'd shift the blame onto her by saying, "If you were the Proverbs 31 woman you teach other women about, you wouldn't be thinking about ending your marriage. You would be able to trust God that I would get it together." He was basically telling her that their marriage was bad because her faith was weak.

Clarissa bought his words. She cried out in her journal as she prayed to God, asking how she could be a better wife and where she had gone wrong. She allowed his words to beat her up. Although utterly untrue, his words affected her profoundly. For a while, she began to doubt herself. His words and the stress of the dying relationship threw her into a depression that led to severe weight loss and other physical ailments.

Clarissa didn't realize she was suffering from emotional abuse until she stumbled across a book about the issue. As she read it, the signs and symptoms she experienced exploded from the page.

Clarissa shook herself awake once she realized that the spoken messages she received from her husband were not true. They were accusatory messages meant to shift the blame away from his own irresponsibility and place the shame of their broken relationship on her.

The entire time you have been reading this section, you have already been evaluating the messages that have been spoken into your life. Whether they are the words you heard as a little girl or what you hear now, spoken messages have great impact. Your current life location may be related to your understanding of the spoken messages you received throughout your life. They could be why you are settling for leeks and onions instead of enjoying milk and honey.

Did you receive positive spoken messages in your life as a child?

If so, how was the element of the spoken message passed to you?

How do you plan to pass it along to your children or loved ones?

If not, how did Satan pervert the spoken message in your life as a child?

Begin speaking positive messages into your own life. Use God's Word as the catalyst for some positive messages. Start each morning for the next month by repeating these truths of Scripture to yourself:

I am the righteousness of God in Christ (2 Cor. 5:21).

I am valuable to God (1 Cor. 6:20).

I belong to Jesus Christ (3:23).

I have amazing promises straight from God (2 Cor. 7:1).

God will never leave me (Heb. 13:5).

My salvation is sure (Eph. 1:13).

## Part 3: Evaluating the Attachment of High Value

Spoken messages also communicate *value*. Several biblical people received such messages. Ruth honored her mother-in-law. Ruth left everything she knew to stay with the widowed and now-childless Naomi. There is no higher value that you can attach to someone other than putting your life on hold while you walk with that person through his or her problems. (See the Book of Ruth.)

We communicate value to others when we affirm their redeeming qualities. There is something good in most people. Find it and let them know you see it.

I do this intentionally with my children. I tell them personally what I appreciate about them, and I let them hear me tell other people how proud I am of who they are. Yes, I'm proud of their accomplishments, but I also want them to know I'm excited about who they are as people. They are wonderful human beings, and they are valuable whether or not they meet the world's standard of success.

I love communicating value to my husband too. James works at a job that can be perilous, so I wrote him a note once thanking him for working so hard and being careful to keep himself safe so he can come home to us every night. When I went into his office months later, I observed that note pinned up on his bulletin board. Out of all the little notes I have left for him, that one meant a lot. Why? In essence, that note says that I value him.

God honored the Israelite people by singling them out as special to Him. This is why God saw it as a rejection when they wanted a king. You see, the proper reaction to honor and value is gratitude. Instead, the Israelites didn't understand that God had elevated them in order to have a closer relationship with them.

This reaction is an example of how Satan perverts messages of honor and value. Satan replaces your gratitude with jealousy. You begin to look *out* at what everybody else has rather than to look *in* at what you already have. The Israelites had God as their King, but the other nations had human royalty, so that's what they wanted instead.

Jealousy is a leeks-and-onions issue. The Bible has only negative things to say about it. For example, Prov. 14:30 says, "A heart at peace gives life to the body, but envy rots the bones," and 1 Cor. 3:3 says, "You are still worldly. For since there is jealousy and quarreling among you, are you not worldly? Are you not acting like mere men?" There are several truths about jealousy we need to know.

Jealousy is a waste of time. When you are jealous, you spend so much time trying to pull the other person down that you take your focus off of your own value and off of the value of the other person. What's so ridiculous is that while you are spinning your wheels being jealous of a sister in Christ, she is probably getting on with life, but you can't move forward because of how you feel about her.

One year I was speaking at a women's retreat, and I reached a point in my talk where I sensed the Holy Spirit telling me to stop and have the ladies pray about personal issues they were having with one another. This idea wasn't on my notes, but obediently—although with trepidation—I told the ladies what I felt God wanted us to do. Then I stepped away from the microphone and bowed my head.

No one moved at first, and then I began to hear feet stepping lightly across the floor. When I looked up, several ladies were approaching others, taking their hands, looking into their eyes, and talking softly.

To my surprise, my friend Vivian (not her real name) was walking toward me. She took my hands in hers and began to ask for my forgiveness of her jealousy toward me. *What?* I thought. *Vivian is one of the holiest women I know. No way is she saying this to me. If anything, I should be jealous of her!* But no, it was true. Vivian and I had been part of a Bible study together and due to circumstances beyond my control I had had to leave the study for several months. When I returned, Vivian said she was jealous because I hadn't seemed to miss a beat. My Bible college background had equipped me with a pretty decent knowledge of God's Word, and she had been struggling to know and understand the things I seemed to grasp effortlessly. She felt there was no need for her to study so hard if Sharon was back with all the answers.

You see, for a short time, Vivian allowed Satan to sow the seed of jealousy and make her feel small and devalued. What a waste of time that was! Instead of fretting about me, she could have enjoyed sweet fellowship in the Word with God. And all that time, I was going about my merry way, preparing for our Bible study times, enjoying being back with the ladies, and not even knowing what Vivian was going through.

Jealousy is very unbecoming. You've heard the saying "Green is just not your color!" Well, I remember when baseball great Sammy Sosa hit homerun number 63. He was playing in an away game and they honored the achievement by flashing congratulatory remarks on the stadium's JumboTron screen. The next day, the newspaper reported that the home team was disgruntled because their home field made such a fuss over an opposing player's hit. Talk about sour grapes! The man deserved the honor; let him have his moment in the sun.

Did you receive a blessing because someone valued you by speaking words of honor? If not, that lack could be a factor in your decision-making process and in understanding your present location in life. Evaluate that area now.

Did you feel you were highly valued in your childhood?

If so:

How did you receive that message?

How do you plan to pass the message of value and honor along to your children or loved ones?

If not:

How did Satan pervert your value in your life as a child?

Thank God now for the high value He has placed upon you. Start by recognizing that He valued you so highly that He died for you (Rom. 5:8) and believe that you are a priceless gem to Him (Prov. 31:10).

Also, start pulling the weeds of jealousy Satan has planted to choke out your high value. Deliberately thank God for the successes you see others enjoy. You may even feel so inclined as to send a congratulatory card to someone who accomplishes something you wish you could have done, like graduating from college, starting a business, getting mar-

ried, or having a baby. After all, we are admonished to rejoice with those who rejoice (Rom. 12:15).

## Part 4: Evaluating a Special Future

The fourth element of a family blessing is picturing a *special future* for the individual being blessed.

God had a wonderful way of picturing special futures for
people in the Bible. Several examples come to mind.

God's promise to Abraham is the classic case of the be-
stowing of a special future. Just having God say He's blessing
him would have been enough for Abraham, but then God
went on to tell him he'd be a great nation, God would have
his back concerning other's responses to him, and all—
count 'em—all the families of the entire earth would be
blessed through him. (See Gen. 12:2-3.)

You'd think Abraham would never mess up since God
promised him a special future, but that was not the case.
Abraham made some mistakes along the way, but God
stayed true to His word. You see, the great thing about
God's promises is that they are sure. God never breaks His
promises. What happens is we short-circuit the benefits of
those promises by our disobedience.

God encouraged Solomon with a special future because
his heart was humble. When Solomon became king, God
gave him carte blanche and asked him what he wanted.
Solomon asked for an understanding heart to judge the
people rightly. God was so pleased that He not only made
Solomon the wisest man who would ever live but also gave
him riches, honor, and long life. (See 1 Kings 3:9-14.)

Mary of Bethany is probably my favorite Bible woman,
and Jesus gave her a special future in response to her act of
love in anointing His feet. (See Mark 14:3-9.) Even though
the men in attendance mumbled under their breath about

what she was doing, He shut them up by pronouncing her special future. "Verily I say unto you, Wheresoever this gospel shall be preached throughout the whole world, this also that she hath done shall be spoken of for a memorial of her" (v. 9, KJV). Mary will always be remembered for her love for the Master.

What do we learn from the above examples of Abraham, Solomon, and Mary? We learn that God encourages His people with special futures. Because He places high value on us, He expects great things for us and from us.

From the time they were born, I wanted to know what God had placed in my children so that I could partner with God and guide them to the future He had planned for them. Besides the Bible, I read several books that helped me in this most crucial endeavor. One book that helped a lot was *You and Your Child* by Charles Swindoll. In it, he explains the meaning of Prov. 22:6 this way: "'Train up a child in the way he should go (and in keeping with his individual gift or bent), and when he is old he will not depart from it.' In every child God places in our arms, there is a bent, a set of characteristics already established . . . The parent who is wise and sensitive comes to know the way God made the child, then fits his training accordingly."[2]

I read another book that encouraged parents to determine what kind of temperament or personality their children had. I discovered that Matthew was a melancholy/choleric, a deep-thinking, take-charge perfectionist. Those personality traits appeared when he was a tiny infant. For his first two weeks, absolutely nothing was right. He cried when he was wet, and he cried when I changed him. He cried when he was hungry, then he cried when he was too full. He fussed when I dressed him, and he fussed when I undressed him. Things were only really cool for him while he was nursing and when he was asleep.

Gradually he gained some control of his world and decided he could trust me to meet his needs. Soon he started school and now he's 18 years old. He's gone through school as the deep-thinking, take-charge perfectionist God made him to be. He organized work teams to produce stellar group projects, he served as student body president in both middle and high school, and any grade less than an A disappoints him. He's graduating high school as class valedictorian and will move into college as a film major. Of course, he wants to be the head honcho, the director of television productions and major motion pictures. Above all, he loves God and has always put his faith first in everything.

By the time my second son, Mark, was born, I had read *Raising Christians, Not Just Children* by Florence Littauer.[3] This book gave me even more direction pertaining to how my own personality traits meshed with my children's. Matthew and I are a lot alike, but knowing myself better helped me relax with Mark's character traits because they are so different from my own.

Mark is my sanguine. Actually, he's a double sanguine if there is such a thing. He's extremely charismatic and funny, the life of the party. He's also very cool and never in a hurry. Too much effort takes the fun out of life, and he doesn't intend to miss a minute's enjoyment.

Again, early on, I recognized these traits. He slept through the night almost from day one and smiled his way through every day and into everyone's heart. He's a great actor and a charmer. He even had his kindergarten teacher fooled into thinking he could read when he actually memorized the pages someone read to him.

Everything he tried came easily to him, especially sports. He's a natural athlete. He can throw a perfect spiral in football, swim like a fish, and dribble, shoot, and steal with the best in basketball. This child is on his way to the NBA or a career in broadcast journalism. He'll have something to do in the public eye because he is definitely not a person who can work behind a desk for eight hours a day.

Knowing these things about my children helps me encourage them to set meaningful goals, goals that are attainable for their special futures because God placed specific talents within them.

I continually communicate to my boys that God has special futures for them. I say things like, *"When* you go to college . . ."* and *"When* you have your own house and are responsible for your own family . . ."* and *"When* you own your own company . . ."* There is never a thought of *if,* only *when* something is going to happen. Now, as older teenagers, my boys are saying these things about themselves.

Satan perverts God's special future when he causes you to stumble with temptation. Then he riddles you with guilt when you fall. Satan will offer distractions and temptations —hoping to get you off God's path. If you bite, you'll have a setback. Then Satan will gladly be right there to heap on guilt nice and thick. You begin wallowing in the guilt and pretty soon you have either forgotten all about the path you were on or you're so discouraged that you think you can never get going again.

Initial guilt is good; it's actually called conviction. You should feel bad when you yield to temptation and sin. Once you realize that you have sinned against God, confess immediately and do whatever you have to do to get up and keep moving forward with your life. A sure sign of spiritual maturity is the short time span between the commission of sin and the confession of it.

After you have confessed your sin before God, the need for conviction is over. Any remaining guilt is of the leeks-and-onions variety. Sniff it out and get rid of it.

Were you given the element of a special future? If not, the temptations to which you've yielded may have resulted in leeks-and-onions guilt that has kept you from experiencing your milk-and-honey blessings.

Did someone communicate that God had a special future for you?

If yes:

How was this picture of a special future passed to you?

How do you plan to pass it along to your children or loved ones?

If no:

How did Satan pervert God's future for your life as a child?

Rejoice over Jer. 29:11. It says, "'For I know the plans I have for you,' declares the LORD, 'plans to prosper you and not to harm you, plans to give you hope and a future.'" Ask God what specific plans He has for you. Then follow your heart while listening for Him to check as you move along the way. Be encouraged by Ps. 37:23-24, "The steps of a good man are ordered by the LORD: and he delighteth in his way. Though he fall, he shall not be utterly cast down: for the LORD upholdeth him with his hand" (KJV).

# Part 5: Evaluating Active Commitment

The fifth and final element of the family blessing goes beyond a spoken message with an *active commitment*.

God has always taken an active commitment in the lives of those He loves. Let's go back to our friends, the Israelites. God was actively committed to getting them out of their bondage under the Egyptian Pharaoh. The 10 plagues were His idea. The Passover was His idea. The parting of the Red Sea, again, was His idea. He played a personal, active role in doing for them what needed to be done to bring about their deliverance.

An even greater example of God showing active commitment is how He orchestrated our deliverance from sin, death, and hell. Jesus literally took our sin on himself, took our punishment, triumphed over it, and now offers us His spotless record that we might have access to God the Father. And all of that wasn't easy. The Cross was no picnic. The sheer agony so vividly and expertly depicted in Mel Gibson's movie *The Passion of the Christ* made the true meaning of the celebration of Easter come into focus for many Christians.

Having an active commitment means you do everything possible to help the one blessed to be successful. Helping that person is not an afterthought or just something you do in your spare time. A big part of your life is wrapped up in helping the one you are blessing.

Good parents know what active commitment takes. My parents were great at exemplifying this element in my life in many ways. One example is their commitment to my musical training.

My grandmother discovered that I had a musical gift. She said I sat down at our family piano when I was 5 years old and picked out combinations of notes until they harmonized. She and my parents then started me on piano lessons. For the next 11 years, every Thursday, my mother took me to Mrs.

Dolly Perry's guest-house-turned-piano-studio and paid for my half-hour classical piano lessons. And every day when I got home from school, Grandma listened as I practiced for 30 minutes before I went outside to play or do anything else.

Even today I love playing the piano. It became my escape when I felt bad, my associate when I felt good, and my companion when I felt lonely. I've even gone on to worship God with my skill at the piano by writing praise songs, leading choirs, and playing for praise and worship at church. My parents' commitment to build my talent added this very special part to my life.

We easily understand what it means to be actively committed to the lives of our children, but we can show active commitment in other areas of our lives as well. In marriage, we can help our spouses realize their dreams. At work, we can participate as a team player so a coworker can be promoted. As a neighbor, we can join the neighborhood watch group or help care for elderly residents on our block.

Satan's perversion of active commitment is workaholism, overcommitment, mixed-up priorities. The man who neglects his family to make more and more money on his job has his priorities askew. No one is saying he shouldn't work at all; he should. The point is there must be a balance. A wife needs her husband and children need their father present. The family will probably fight over the money when he's gone, but they'll fondly remember the times they all spent doing things together.

Parents can also get carried away with commitment. You've heard the phrase "too much of a good thing," right? Some parents have no lives of their own apart from their children. It's important for parents to also set aside time to nurture their marriage relationship and their personal relationship with the Lord.

My friend Jean recently told me about her concern for her daughter who had been neglecting church attendance, using her child's involvement in sports as her excuse. Jean pointed out to her daughter that if she could make time to attend every practice, every game, and every team party, she could make time to go to church. In her diligence to show her son that she was committed to his activities, her daughter was neglecting her more important task of teaching her son that commitment to God should take precedence over everything else in his life.

Workaholism, overcommitment, mixed-up priorities: all are leeks-and-onions problems that could have been precipitated as Satan sought to pervert the element of active commitment in your life. Your current location might be the result of decisions you have made or attitudes you hold because you did not have someone actively committed to cheering you on.

If no one has ever taken an active commitment in your life, realize that God has. He took personal interest in you, bankrupting heaven to send His own Son to die so that you might live. Once you believe what God has done, bolster your own confidence in yourself. My husband says, "It's a poor dog that doesn't wag its own tail." Even if no one else is committed to you, be committed to yourself. Return to school for that degree, go for that promotion, launch that dream business, or write that book.

Did you receive the active commitment element of the family blessing in your life as a child?

If yes:

How was the element of active commitment passed to you?

How do you plan to pass it along to your children or loved ones?

If no:

How did Satan pervert the element of active commitment in your life as a child?

Write out a specific plan to deal with your workaholism, over-commitment, or mixed-up priorities. Act on some part of your plan this week. Then determine to make further changes regularly, perhaps implementing some small change every other week until you form new habits.

# Six

# Obstructions

## What Is Hindering My Deliverance?

We have examined our lives against the backdrop of the journey of the Israelite people into the Promised Land, and we are ready to expose the obstructions that keep us from cleansing our Egyptian palates. Once we tear down these walls and climb out of these ruts, we will be ready to move into our personal promised lands—the milk-and-honey blessings God has in store for us.

The things that hold us back are very similar to the obstructions the Israelites faced when they were about to step into their milk-and-honey future.

## Obstruction 1: Rebellion

After delivering the Ten Commandments and the Law at Mount Sinai, God directed the Israelites to the threshold of the Promised Land. Numbers 13 and 14 recounts the story.

First, God told Moses to send some men across the border to check out the land. (See Num. 13:2.) So Moses chose 12 men and sent them into the Promised Land. God told them to "search the land" and Moses gave them additional instructions:

When Moses sent them to explore Canaan he said, "Go up through the Negev and on into the hill country. See what the land is like and whether the people who live there are strong or weak, few or many. What kind of land do they live in? Is it good or bad? What kind of towns do they live in? Are they unwalled or fortified? How is the soil? Is it fertile or poor? Are there trees on it or not? Do your best to bring back some of the fruit of the land." (It was the season for the first ripe grapes) (vv. 17-20).

So away went the exploratory team. They walked around in Canaan (which is the map name for the Promised Land) for 40 days. As proof of how phenomenal the land was, they cut down a cluster of grapes so huge that it took two of them to carry it back to the Israelite camp.

The first words out of the search party's mouths were, "We went into the land to which you sent us, and it does flow with milk and honey! Here is its fruit" (v. 27).

I can almost hear the exited murmur roll through the crowd as they started to talk excitedly about moving.

And then came the dreaded word. *But . . .*

I can imagine time slowing, first for Moses and then for the rest of the people. *Did they say "but"? There's not supposed to be a "but." There's only supposed to be the instruction to pack up.*

Unfortunately, Moses and all the people heard it right. The search team was saying, "But . . ." There was a problem. If this were a made-for-TV movie, it would cut to a commercial right here, making the audience wait awhile, giving us a chance to ruminate and try to digest the implications of this unexpected twist. After the commercial break, the search team would finish its report.

Except this was no movie. The team continued, "But the people who live there are powerful, and the cities are fortified and very large. We even saw descendants of Anak there. The Amalekites live in the Negev; the Hittites, Jebusites and Amorites live in the hill country; and the Canaanites live near the sea and along the Jordan" (vv. 28-29).

*Houston, we have a problem.* All that time, all that travel, all that waiting only brought them to fortified cities inhabited by and surrounded by powerful people.

Then up spoke a voice of reason. "Then Caleb silenced the people before Moses and said, 'We should go up and take possession of the land, for we can certainly do it'" (v. 30).

Now we're getting somewhere. At least one of the discovery team had faith. Unfortunately, that dreaded word was thrown back into the mix.

"But the men who had gone up with him said, 'We can't attack those people. . . . The land we explored devours those living in it. . . . We seemed like grasshoppers in our own eyes, and we looked the same to them'" (vv. 31-33).

It's important to fully understand God's directions, so let's dissect the original instructions. The word for "explore," in both God's directions to Moses and Moses' directions to the men, comes from the Hebrew word *tuwr* (toor), which means "to meander about, especially for trade or reconnoitering." Reconnoitering basically means to recognize and to engage in reconnaissance. Reconnaissance means "a preliminary survey to gain information; especially an exploratory military survey of enemy territory." All these guys were supposed to do was look, check things out, and bring back some precise information about the land. No one asked them to make a judgment as to whether or not they would be able to take it over.

So what did they do? They came back with a judgment about whether or not they could take it over, and they decided against God's promise that He would give them the land. Although God had promised to give the land to them, it wouldn't become theirs until they took it, and they decided not to. They didn't get what they were given because they refused to take it.

How in the world did the Israelites allow themselves to get into that predicament?

First, the assembly of the Israelites listened to the wrong people. They listened to people who put their own ideas ahead of God's word and desires. This is the essence of rebellion, not doing what you know you're supposed to do.

Second, they reacted to the wrong message. They refused to go into the land because of a report that contradicted God's word.

The same problem of rebellion hinders your deliverance today. You rebel when you listen to the wrong people. Then you slip into deeper rebellion when you react to their wrong message. Therefore, in order to avoid hindrances to your deliverance, guard your vision. Protect it from the influence of the wrong people. Second, think carefully before you respond. Be sure you react only in the direction of God's leading.

## Guard Your Vision

Sending the search team is like sharing your vision with others. Moses sent the search team to see what God knew was already there. When you share your vision with others, you share what God has put on your heart. You bring those people onto your team—let them into your confidence. You say to them, "You are important enough for me to let you in on a secret that, until now, has been only between God and me." Know this, my friends: You can't share your vision with everybody. Although you are excited about what God has said to you, not everybody else will be. Folks who just don't get your dreams and who don't share the enthusiasm about your visions are folks who try to do something to prevent you from realizing them. Those people are known, in current teen vernacular, as "haters," an appropriate term, and you'll soon see why.

At 15, my friend Tammy didn't understand she was following God's call for her life. All she was sure of was the strong urge she felt toward becoming a teacher. She taught successfully for some years before she realized that her high school English teacher was a "hater." When Tammy told Mrs. Simms that she wanted to enter the teaching profession, Mrs. Simms recited a litany of reasons why Tammy would never become one. Tammy endured a speech about her laziness and her lack of the commitment and patience necessary for the profession. This woman who was supposed to be an encourager even threw in a racial slur about Tammy ending up "like all the rest" of her race's lost causes.

Mrs. Simms did not believe in Tammy's *ability* to reach her goals. When someone discounts your capability or motivation after God clearly reveals His mind to you, that person is a hater. Move past that person and remember that he or she is not someone with whom you should share God's vision for you.

Another type of hater is the person who doesn't believe your vision. This is the person who tells you you're making it up. This person questions the authenticity of your message from the Lord.

Nathaniel is a good example. After Jesus' baptism, people started following Him, believing Him to be the promised Lamb of God about whom John the Baptist had been foretelling. Philip was one of those first followers. Those guys were so excited about spreading the news about Jesus to their friends; you know, like when we tell our girlfriends about a great sale. Well, Philip excitedly told Nathaniel, "We have found him, of whom Moses in the law, and the prophets, did write, Jesus of Nazareth, the son of Joseph" (John 1:45, KJV).

Nathaniel was a *disbelieving* hater. He responded, "Can there any good thing come out of Nazareth?" (v. 46, KJV). You see, Nathaniel did not believe what Philip had come to know about Jesus. He did not catch the vision, so he responded with doubt. In essence, Nathaniel was saying, "You cannot really believe that you have found the Messiah, especially not from Nazareth."

Some of the followers believed and some didn't. Those who did were people whose spirits resonated in harmony with those who shared the vision. Their response was, "Yes, I feel the same way you feel." If you receive the opposite response from someone with whom you have shared your vision, you are dealing with the disbelieving hater.

The third type of discourager is the *jealous* hater. This person doesn't want you to get ahead. He or she is jealous of your probable success. The age-old crabs-in-a-barrel example illustrates this type. I've heard that if crabs have been captured and are on the way to their deaths, they will not allow any of the other crabs to climb out of the barrel. If any free-thinking crab tries to escape, those on the bottom will yank the climber back down.

Jealous haters are yankers. They will do their best to yank your excitement, yank your joy, and yank the wind right out of your sails by keeping you from attaining the success that pursuing your vision will mean. These are the people who don't want you to get the promotion, start that business, or write that book.

"Look at all the extra time you'll have to spend at the office," they'll say. "You deserve to have that time free for yourself."

"Who wants all the headaches of management?" they'll argue. "It's so much less hassle to be right where you are, here with the rest of us. Do you really think you can command the respect of the office personnel? Girl, that's not even you!"

"Write a book? That's pretty highfalutin talk, thinking

that folks will really be all that interested in what you have to say."

When the jealous hater opens her big mouth, close your ears. She's not there with constructive criticism or wise counsel. She uses calculated words to keep you in your place.

Do not bring haters into your confidence. They will do their best to discourage and dissuade you. If you decide to listen to haters rather than God, you will shortchange yourself and miss out on the best God intends for you. If the people you allow into your vision are not on board with God, what they have to say could foster discouragement in you and begin to lead you in the wrong direction. Advice not based on God's principles is always bad advice. What may be a perfectly fine suggestion for someone else or for some other circumstance may not be right for you.

However, do not confuse haters with friends who are genuinely trying to help you—wise counselors who are legitimately suggesting that you think things through. The acquaintance who points out that you faint at the sight of blood is not an ability-hater when she tells you that you may be on the wrong track if you desire to become an emergency room nurse. If you have a new vision this month that cancels out the vision you had last month, don't call your friend a disbelieving hater if she's slow to jump on this new bandwagon.

With whom do you share your deliverance visions?

What are the following verses speaking to you about guarding your vision, accepting counsel, and avoiding haters?

"Turn you at my reproof: behold, I will pour out my spirit unto you, I will make known my words unto you" (Prov. 1:23, KJV).

"And I will put my spirit within you, and cause you to walk in my statutes, and ye shall keep my judgments, and do them" (Ezek. 36:27, KJV).

"Where no counsel is, the people fall: but in the multitude of counsellors there is safety" (Prov. 11:14, KJV).

"Plans fail for lack of counsel, but with many advisers they succeed" (15:22).

"Perfume and incense bring joy to the heart, and the pleasantness of one's friend springs from his earnest counsel" (27:9).

## Gauge Your Response

After you have made sure you have properly guarded your vision, it's time to gauge your response. It's natural to feel all excited right after you hear from God. It's also natural to wonder soon after, "Now, did I really hear from God or was it just my imagination?" To gauge your response means to be careful to keep God's vision before you and be sure you respond only in the direction of God's leading.

The Israelites were sure of their vision; they understood it from the day they left Egypt. *Moses says that God is taking us to the Promised Land.* They weren't exactly sure where the Promised Land was, but they headed out anyway. Unfortunately, it didn't take long nor did it take much pressure before they began to lose sight of the vision, to doubt whether Moses' message was right. Several times hardships arose and they murmured against Moses. They accused him of delivering them from bondage just to have them die out in no-man's land.

Losing sight of the milk-and-honey promise sets the stage for rebellion. Seeds of discouragement brought on by hardship need only a little fertilizer to blossom into full-blown insurgence. The Israelites didn't guard their vision by holding fast to what God had said. Instead, they listened to the negative report of the search team. Now the rebellion could fully grow and thrive as they reacted incorrectly to the bad counsel they received. They decided to respond in fear and believe the report of those who went against God's plan. They second-guessed God and lost.

There's a difference between not being sure of what God has said and second-guessing Him. Nothing's wrong with being uncertain; everything's wrong with being uncooperative. God did not punish people for asking Him, "God, was that really You?" For example, when Gabriel told Mary she was going to have a baby who would be the Messiah, she questioned the announcement. (See Luke 1:31-34.) Gideon, a judge of God's people, wanted to be sure he had heard from God and asked God to prove the message not one way, but two. (See Judg. 6:36-40.)

When you're not sure if you've heard from God, stop and ask Him. Search the Word, pray, seek godly counsel, put out a fleece. God created logic, so He uses it. Think about it. What sense would it make for God to want you to do something and then hide from you what it is that He wants? God desires that you know Him and follow Him. You can depend upon Him to show His will to you clearly.

When God speaks, He will confirm His word with whatever signs you need. Jesus worked with His first disciples this way. Since He is the same yesterday, today, and forever, He still works with us this way. (See Mark 16:19-20.)

Once you are sure of what God wants you to do, get moving. Walk confidently into the vision. You disobey and sin if you don't. It is your responsibility to follow the deliverance vision God gives you. God doesn't need anybody else's help to deliver you. However, as we saw in the last section, He can use other people who are in tune with Him to give you guidance about handling the specifics of working out the vision. Remember how the wise men shared with Herod their vision about their search for the King? (See Matt. 2.) They were following their vision and they had no idea that Herod would not be as excited about the news of the new King as they were. God stepped in with new direction—further instruction that would actually protect their vision, telling them to return to their country without returning to Herod.

How should you gauge your response when God gives you a vision? Confer with God in prayer and with wise counselors He's provided in your life. Then take the next logical step. God won't lay out every detail of the vision all at once. You probably couldn't handle it. Just do the next logical thing.

I'm in the process of starting a new business. Some years ago I discovered my spiritual teaching gift and began using it. I teach the Word to women and teens through conference speaking and writing books, articles, and devotions. As I moved forward in those areas, opportunities opened for me to teach beginning writers to start their own writing ministries. People who take my workshops at conferences tell me their lives have been changed and their writing revolutionized.

I love teaching these workshops so much that I began to ask the Lord if this was something I should launch into on my own. I believe my love for this teaching, the gift God's given, and others' responses have combined to help me hear God's call. I shared this vision with my husband, my spiritual leader and a very practical man. After he listened to my idea, he said, "Go for it, Baby."

So I brainstormed the idea with another friend who is good at putting vision down on paper. Then we came up with the business name—AuthorizeMe. I contacted the governmental office in my state and obtained the legal paperwork to do business in that name, then secured my Web site. The business plan is being drafted and the first workshops are tentatively slotted. I even have flyers and business cards—via my own desktop computer—ready to hand out to everyone I talk with about the business.

You see, the vision of AuthorizeMe is growing and evolving. God knows the end; I don't. I have gauged my reaction to the vision. I'm excited, but I'm not quitting my day job just yet. Each time I take one step, I simply continue by taking the next logical step.

Rebellion is the result of losing sight of God's vision and then not following through. Rebellion is a hindrance because it keeps you from doing what you must do to realize God's vision. The vision is God's prepared meal; rebellion is your refusal to pick up the utensils and eat. React to a meal this way and you will starve. React to a vision this way and you won't see it come to fruition.

What is the vision you feel God has given you?


What scriptures or confirmation have you received to help you know this vision is of God?

How are you gauging your response? What steps are you taking toward the fulfillment of that vision?

## Obstruction 2: The Wilderness

The second obstruction to deliverance is a wilderness. Merriam-Webster's online dictionary defines a wilderness as "a tract or region uncultivated and uninhabited by human beings, an empty or pathless area or region." The Hebrew word for *wilderness* used in Num. 14 means desert, a place where things were consumed, a place where things die.

A wilderness is not a place where most people want to be. It's a place you avoid. On the cross-country driving trips my family took every summer, the longest part was the trek from the California desert through Texas. All that open land was unbearably hot, dry, and lonely—the closest to a wilderness I ever want to get. We always breathed a collective, relieved sigh once we got through the desert and began seeing trees again. Just imagine what a miserable vacation it would have been if we never got out of that wilderness—if we never arrived at our "promised land"—our vacation destination.

The Israelites experienced a wilderness that kept them from making it to the Promised Land. Consider the following two points about their wilderness wandering, and let's draw some parallels with our own wildernesses.

First, the wilderness the Israelites found themselves in was one they had already experienced. From the time they crossed the Red Sea until the time they reached Kadesh-Barnea, they had been in the wilderness. During that trip, God took them to Mount Sinai where they received His Law. Then He led them to the threshold of their blessing.

God showed them all they needed to learn about Him during that trip. He could miraculously deliver (the parting of the Red Sea), He could miraculously protect (drowning the Egyptian army), He could miraculously provide (water from a rock), He could miraculously sustain (manna from heaven), He could miraculously lead (pillars of cloud and fire), and He could miraculously rule (Ten Commandments written by the finger of God). That wilderness crossing may have seemed tough, but God was teaching them—getting them ready for how to trust Him once they came into their blessing.

The first time through the wilderness was for their preparation; the second time was their punishment. To illustrate: When I discipline my children, I intend to have to tell them something only once. When I'm sure they understand, if I have to tell them again, there's going to be trouble.

When the negative report frightened the Israelites, they refused to go into the Promised Land. God was so displeased that He declared none of that generation, except Joshua and Caleb, would live to go in. They would all die. Guess where? In the wilderness. That's right. They would have to wander around in circles for 40 years, until all the old, disbelieving geezers died off. Read the account in Num. 14:29-35.

Your wilderness is an obstruction, keeping you from your promised land, if you are going through it because you didn't obey or learn your lesson the first time. There's nothing you can do about this except go through it. Humbly submit to whatever it is God wants you to learn.

Second, your wilderness will cost others. The young Israelites had to suffer with the old. "Your children will be shepherds here for forty years, suffering for your unfaithfulness, until the last of your bodies lies in the desert" (v. 33). Thanks to the decisions of the adults, the children had to wander around for 40 years having funerals.

An old saying declares, "No man is an island." You do not live in a vacuum. Your life touches others, so when you mess up and get punished, everyone around you is affected. It's sort of like the computer game called Minesweeper. Every number touches another number, a blank space, or a bomb. In the game, you try to open up the numbers and mark the bombs. If by mistake you click a space that is a bomb, you lose. You basically blow up the rest of the board.

The husband who gambles away his money displaces his wife and kids when they lose the house. The woman who has an affair destroys her reputation in front of her daughter. The few kids who are caught cheating on a test cause the whole class to suffer if the teacher decides to give a different, more difficult test.

When you bomb, those around you suffer. I know this is going to sound simplistic, but think about what you are going to do before you do it. How will your actions affect your spouse, your children, your parents, your siblings, your friends, and your coworkers? How will your actions affect the Church? Will you be an embarrassment to our Lord Jesus Christ?

God provided manna for the Israelites for the entire 40 years of wilderness wandering, but it was a sad time. His compassion extended to them even though He was punishing them. I was loving my sons even when I had to spank them. As a matter of fact, I was spanking them because I loved them. Hebrews 12:7-8 instructs us in this manner, "Endure hardship as discipline; God is treating you as sons. For what son is not disciplined by his father? If you are not disciplined (and everyone undergoes discipline), then you are illegitimate children and not true sons."

You may be in a wilderness right now. Oswald Chambers, in *My Utmost for His Highest,* has some great advice. In the

April 26 entry, he says, "If you will remain true to God, God will lead you straight through every barrier into the inner chamber of the knowledge of Himself."[1] Whether your wilderness is a matter of preparation or punishment, be a quick study and learn what God is trying to teach you. Stop struggling against the lesson. You can come out of the wilderness with your palate totally cleansed of leeks-and-onions taste—totally ready for the milk and honey of your promised land.

Identify the wilderness you are now in.


How have you been fighting against the discipline?


Say a prayer now determining to humble yourself under God's hand of discipline.

# Seven

# Emancipation
What Part Do I Play in My Deliverance?

Ladies, congratulate yourselves. You have successfully completed the discovery part of this book. Aren't you excited? You should be. If you've actually taken the hard looks I've suggested, you have learned quite a bit about yourself. I know it isn't always easy to acknowledge what we actually see. But that's OK. You have lived through it.

Now it's time to get down to the business of moving forward. These last chapters will also require work on your part, but it's always more fun building and decorating the structure than digging in the dirt to pour the foundation. You have finished the hard foundation work, the work that took place in the dark, on the inside. Now let's build up and out.

God has sent His Word to deliver us from whatever situation, problem, test, or trial we face. God's Word illuminates all our dark places—all our bondage situations. We will not escape without Him as our Deliverer, and we will not know how the deliverance will be played out without His Word.

God has always operated via His Word. All through the creation story, everything happened because of God's word. Eleven times in Gen. 1, we are told, "And God said." What we know as reality was brought into being by God's word.

We learn more about God's word in the first chapter of the Gospel of John, which begins by saying, "In the beginning was the Word, and the Word was with God, and the Word was God. He was with God in the beginning. Through him all things were made; without him nothing was made that has been made. In him was life, and that life was the light of men" (vv. 1-4). Verse 14 finishes the thought by essentially telling us that the Word being referred to is none other than Jesus Christ.

So you see, God's Word is always creative, but in addition to that, it is life-giving. Notice that the Word not only gives us life; it gives us light. Matthew Henry's commentary explains this point as follows:

> The spirit of a man is the candle of the Lord, and it was the eternal Word that lighted this candle. The light of reason, as well as the life of sense, is derived from him, and depends upon him. This proves him fit to undertake our salvation; for life and light, spiritual and eternal life and light, are the two great things that fallen man, who lies so much under the power of death and darkness, has need of. From whom may we better expect the light of divine revelation than from him who gave us the light of human reason?[1]

What's the point? The point is that God's Word, executed through Jesus Christ, has come into our lives to give us direction. The Word lights our way.

The part we play is to act upon the word He gives us relative to our issue. Let's look at four possibilities.

# Part 1: Walk Away

Take into account the example of the Israelites whom we have been following through this book. Thanks to 10 well-designed plagues, God convinced Pharaoh to release His people from their bondage. But Pharaoh's command to leave Egypt would have fallen flat if the Hebrew people did not get up and walk away. The people had a responsibility in the matter.

We give all kinds of excuses as to why we don't simply walk

away from negative circumstances, but in the end, everything we rationalize is still nothing more than an excuse. My husband taught me this lesson while we were dating.

My oldest son, Matthew, went through a stage during middle school in which he wanted to bleach his hair blond. I thought about it and even consulted my hair stylist about any risks that might be involved. After I got all the information, I decided that bleaching his hair wasn't illegal, immoral, or dangerous, so I told him to go ahead. In fact, I accompanied him to the beauty supply store to pick out the hair color, and I helped him apply it.

He looked a little weird and everyone reacted with the shocked surprise I think he intended to arouse. No harm, no foul. But then another adult family member saw him. During a telephone conversation, this person expressed his disapproval coupled with an indictment directed at my ability to be a good mother. Well, I was highly upset, to say the least. I worked myself into quite a state, defending myself and my son. When I hung up, my heart was beating fast and I'm sure my temperature had risen. I dialed James.

He listened to me vent and then said, "You know, you brought all this on yourself."

*What?* I thought. *I can't believe this man is not siding with me on this.*

But I was wrong about my assessment of what James said. He went on to explain that I was in control of whether or not I stayed in that conversation and whether or not I accepted that criticism. There was no need for me to dignify that false accusation and indictment with my energy. It was within my power to simply put that conversation behind me.

You, too, can walk away from certain negative situations in your life. When God opens the doors to freedom, walk through them—don't just stand there looking over into your promised land thinking, "Wow, it sure is nice over there!" Take a walk on over there, honey.

What do the following verses tell you about God's Word and your steps?

"The steps of a good man are ordered by the Lord: and he delighteth in his way" (Ps. 37:23, KJV).

"The law of his God is in his heart; his feet do not slip" (v. 31).

"Direct my footsteps according to your word; let no sin rule over me" (119:133).

"In his heart a man plans his course, but the Lord determines his steps" (Prov. 16:9).

## Part 2: Carry and Labor

In answer to the prayers of Sarah, Hannah, and Elizabeth, God opened the wombs of these heretofore barren biblical women, and they gave birth to healthy babies. The catch was, once these women got pregnant, they actually had to go through the pregnancy. Those of you who have had babies know that that is more than a notion.

There may be times when changing your life will require you to do some carrying and laboring. You may not get off scot-free. Just as these women had to carry and bear these babies, you may experience some anguish in your transformation. Breaking free from old habits can be painful. Bursting through barriers takes some muscle. Facing a fear takes courage.

Rosa Parks, like many African-Americans subjugated to the Jim Crow laws in the South, tired of the injustice racial segregation imposed. Rosa's simple act of keeping her seat on a city bus sparked the Civil Rights Movement that changed America. Arrested and thrown into jail, she worked tirelessly once released to see the changes through. God worked to deliver Black people from injustice, and He used the labor of people like Rosa Parks to bring it all to pass.

There may be some work God has in store for you to do. God deals with you according to what you know you ought to do. Step up to the challenge.

What do these verses tell you about God and His expectations of you and the work you should be carrying out?

"Then hear from heaven, your dwelling place. Forgive, and deal with each man according to all he does, since you know his heart" (2 Chron. 6:30).


"If you say, 'But we knew nothing about this,' does not he who weighs the heart perceive it? Does not he who guards your life know it? Will he not repay each person according to what he has done?" (Prov. 24:12).


"And that you, O Lord, are loving. Surely you will reward each person according to what he has done" (Ps. 62:12).

"Behold, I am coming soon! My reward is with me, and I will give to everyone according to what he has done" (Rev. 22:12).

# Part 3: Take and Raise

It couldn't have been easy for Joseph to learn that Mary was pregnant when he knew he hadn't had intercourse with her. The next news must have been both a relief and a shock. An angelic visit convinced Joseph of the truth of Mary's account of being impregnated by the power of the Holy Spirit. After that, we're told that he took Mary to be his wife. (See Matt. 1:20-25.) If you simply skip from there to the story of Jesus' birth, you miss the humanness of this man.

You see, Matt. 1:25 begins with four very important words concerning Joseph. *"And knew her not* till she had brought forth her firstborn son: and he called his name JE-SUS"* (KJV, emphasis added).

I think it didn't really hit Joseph until later that he would have to wait—not only until the wedding, but another nine months plus the purification period—before he could consummate his marriage. Also, God was asking him to raise a child who was not his own.

Now, you may put Mary and Joseph on a really high pedestal, but when I look at the people in the Bible, one thing is strikingly clear: They were all normal people. They had good days and bad days, rich successes and glaring failures. Joseph was an ordinary man thrust into an extraordinary situation. I suspect his thoughts didn't just jump into spiritual mode automatically, as ours don't when we are thrust into something new and stressful.

God provided Joseph with deliverance from his confu-

sion by giving him specific direction. His deliverance
worked itself out when he stuck with the responsibility he
had been given. Joseph was not necessarily in a bad place,
but he needed deliverance to a better place. In this higher
place, Joseph took and raised this child, God's own Son. No
pressure!

Maybe you're doing just fine right where you are, but
God may want to move you to the next level. If that's the
case, your part is to take on the new responsibility with humility and joy. Your place in the scheme of things may not
be to get all the accolades for yourself. Perhaps, like Joseph,
you are being called to nurture someone else.

How do the following verses speak to your situation if you
sense God prompting you to take and raise something or someone?

"Greater love hath no man than this, that a man lay down his
life for his friends" (John 15:13, KJV).

"He that is faithful in that which is least is faithful also in
much: and he that is unjust in the least is unjust also in much"
(Luke 16:10, KJV).

"For unto whomsoever much is given, of him shall be much required: and to whom men have committed much, of him they
will ask the more" (Luke 12:48, KJV).

# Part 4: Tell Others

After the Crucifixion, Jesus delivered Mary Magdalene from her grief by comforting her with the message that He was alive. Her response to that deliverance was to carry the message to others. This may seem like the perfect part for you to play if you're a talker. However, it's not always easy to tell people what they need to hear.

Samuel was a young man living with the priest Eli. One day, God audibly called to Samuel and what He said was not a nice message. Nevertheless, Samuel told Eli what God said, even though he knew the message would hurt Eli. (See 1 Sam. 3:1-18.)

I have learned valuable lessons about God and about life during difficult situations. I have shared some of those lessons with you in this book. I have shared others through talks and magazine articles. There are still others I hope to share in future volumes. The point is, I believe God walked with me through my trials so that I could come out still glorifying Him and testifying of His power.

God trusted Job even when Satan threw his very worst at him. Will you come out of your troubles with a testimony? I contend that our Christian witness will be stronger if we persevere through our hardships holding God's hand rather than coming to the brink of the hardship and then letting go and running. We go *to*, but we refuse to go *through*. Testimony lies on the other side of *through*.

Ephesians 2:10 tells us, "For we are God's workmanship, created in Christ Jesus to do good works, which God prepared in advance for us to do." God has meticulously crafted us to do His specifically chosen work. What we do, others see. What we say, others hear. May we have the testimony of Peter and John as they addressed the high priest and others upon being reprimanded about preaching Jesus. They said,

"For we cannot but speak the things which we have seen and heard" (Acts 4:20, KJV).

What has God brought you through that can be a testimony?


To walk away, to carry and deliver, to take and raise, to tell others: these are Promised Land activities—staples in a diet of milk and honey. Once you begin to live this way, you will find yourself far from Egypt—far from the place that had you craving leeks and onions. As you develop the habit of cooperating with God, you will be cultivating the taste for the milk-and-honey ways of God. Your palate will no longer tolerate the leeks-and-onions tastes of the world. Each time you look back at Egypt, it will seem farther and farther away. Hallelujah!

# ♨ Eight
# Transformation
What Should I Leave Behind?

I think it's pretty safe to assume that you have experienced moving from one home to another. This event is listed on the "most stressful experience" index.

I moved four years ago when James and I married. I learned that we could not comfortably combine our households until we both got rid of some stuff. For the memorabilia buff in me, the relocation itself wasn't the stressor. What hurt me was leaving things behind. What in the world should I part with? Should I keep my first wedding dress? After all, it was redesigned from my mother's gown. Will my china replace his in the dining room china cabinet? What about the boys' cute elementary school projects? You see my dilemma, right?

Whenever there's a move, what we value most makes the move; the other stuff doesn't.

Now that you are clearly on the threshold of your promised land, start packing to move into your blessing. But you can't take everything with you. So what do you leave behind? Everything you don't absolutely need, everything associated with your old life that might hold you back. In other words, leave behind your taste for leeks and onions—those actions and attitudes that draw your mind to the past and gratify your flesh.

Read Gal. 5:19-21:

The acts of the sinful nature are obvious: sexual immorality, impurity and debauchery; idolatry and witchcraft; hatred, discord, jealousy, fits of rage, selfish ambition, dissensions, factions and envy; drunkenness, orgies, and the like. I warn you, as I did before, that those who live like this will not inherit the kingdom of God.

Even when it's time to move on in God, we tend to carry along the baggage of the sinful nature. Why? Two reasons: First, we are comfortable with what's familiar, and second, we just don't want to let go of the control of our lives.

What we must remember is this: Promised Land dwellers are citizens loyal to the King of Kings. It is not within our rights to do whatever we please any longer; it is only within our rights to do whatever God pleases. But since we are so drawn to the familiar and we don't want to relinquish control, we make excuses for our baggage of actions. No matter how eloquently we may express them, though, they are still just that—excuses.

God's Word clearly expresses His attitude toward each and every one of the above listed "acts of the sinful nature." It's time to get serious about purging sinful practices and attitudes from your life. You've been enjoying those Egyptian delights long enough; now it's time to be an epicure of Promised Land delicacies.

Long before we met, my husband was a two-pack-a-day smoker. He quit in one day. How? He was watching the nightly news and the surgeon general's new report on the hazards of cigarette smoking. Dr. C. Everett Koop said that due to current, irrefutable findings, the warnings on the packages had been changed from "smoking may be hazardous" to "smoking is hazardous to your health."

James was sitting at his kitchen table with a pack of cigarettes in front of him. He picked up the package and read the warning. Sure enough, there was the truth, staring him in the face. He put out the cigarette he was holding, disposed of the package, and said, "Well, then, if I keep smoking, I'm a fool."

*Matthew Henry's Commentary* explains that men and women will never be comfortable as Christians if they continue to "plunge themselves in the filth of the flesh; nor will the righteous and holy God ever admit such into his favour and presence, unless they be first washed and sanctified, and justified in the name of our Lord Jesus, and by the Spirit of our God."[1]

I'm getting ready to figuratively spread these Egyptian delights out on a table in front of you. As you examine how these sinful practices work themselves out in your life, be as honest with yourself about what you are reading as James was about what he learned about cigarettes. Begin immediately to unpack your baggage—to cleanse your palate of your taste for these practices.

## Sins Against the Seventh Commandment

It is our corrupt human nature that produces a longing to participate in this first group of sins: adultery, fornication, uncleanness, and lasciviousness. Admit it, when we give in to sexual impurity it often results in the wrecking of our own marriage or the marriage of others, and innocent adults and children suffer in the process.

Everything God has given us He's given to be enjoyed to its fullest and that includes sexual relationships. But like all good things, sexuality can be misused. I've heard lately that studies have been done showing that consumption of chocolate is good for your heart. But if you misuse that information and eat too much of it, it's not healthy. When you indulge in adultery, fornication, uncleanness, and lasciviousness, you're misusing what God has given you for your enjoyment.

Are you an adulteress? Break off the relationship.

Are you indulging in fornication? Return to celibacy. The Greek word for fornication is *porneia,* from which we get the root of our English word *pornography.* Sex outside of marriage is not the end of this point. It is also wrong to participate vicariously through pornographic magazines, books, movies, and the like.

Do you have a dirty mind? The Greek words for *uncleanness* and *lasciviousness* carry with them the idea not only of physical impropriety but also of moral filth. In other words, your thought life is also subject to this warning.

How do you go about changing your thought life? You change your thought life by programming in better information. GIGO = garbage in; garbage out. Luke 6:45 says it well, "The good man brings good things out of the good stored up in his heart, and the evil man brings evil things out of the evil stored up in his heart. For out of the overflow of his heart his mouth speaks."

Take control of what goes into your head. Use wisdom concerning the television shows and movies you watch and the music you listen to. As for filth that's already in your head, begin to counteract those old thoughts by bombarding yourself with new, godly ones. Romans 12:2 tells you the way to transformation is through renewal of the mind. This is the only way to break free of conformity to the world's way of thinking.

Where do you begin on your new-thinking-idea quest? Try starting with a study of Philippians 4:8: "Finally, brothers, whatever is true, whatever is noble, whatever is right, whatever is pure, whatever is lovely, whatever is admirable— if anything is excellent or praiseworthy—think about such things."

Look around you. What is true, noble, and right? What

things are pure, lovely, and admirable? Start thinking about these things. Replace falsehood with truth, the undignified with the noble, and wrong with right. Substitute the impure with the pure, ugly thoughts with lovely ones, and unworthiness with that which is admirable.

## Sins Against the First and Second Commandments

The next acts of the sinful nature, idolatry and witchcraft, concern making anything else a god in our lives except God. Nothing shows the depravity of the human heart more clearly than participation in a false system that pits itself against the true and living God.

Idolatry is image-worship. What images are you worshiping? When we've grown as Christians for any length of time, we have probably moved past worshiping money, our kids, our husbands, and our possessions. More insidious, though, and often overlooked is one's worship of oneself. That's right; that's what I said. We worship ourselves. We worship the image we have of ourselves as great wives, mothers, businesswomen, and even as great Christians. We can be so busy trying to keep up an image that we spend all our time nurturing that image of ourselves rather than nurturing what God actually wants us to become.

The only way to steer clear of idolatry is to keep your eyes on Jesus. Seek Jesus in prayer and ask Him to show you ways you have participated in idolatry. The following two verses can help you start to overcome it.

"Let us fix our eyes on Jesus, the author and perfecter of our faith" (Heb. 12:2).

"Since, then, you have been raised with Christ, set your hearts on things above, where Christ is seated at the right hand of God. Set your minds on things above, not on earthly things. For you died, and your life is now hidden with Christ in God" (Col. 3:1-3).

Now what about witchcraft? *Surely,* you say, *no woman of God is involved in witchcraft.* Let's not be so quick to gloss over this point. God would not have mentioned it if it wasn't important.

The Greek word used here is *farmakeia,* and it's where we get our English word *pharmacy.* Many times, sorcery and enchantments were accompanied by the use of poisons and medicines. Indeed, God does not intend for us to participate in the obvious practices associated with witchcraft that include going to mediums, having séances, reading Tarot cards, and depending on our astrological forecast. He is also warning us here of the dangers of drug abuse.

Do you have witchcraft issues? Get whatever help you need to make the appropriate changes in your habits.

## Sins Against Our Neighbors

The next sins of the flesh listed are sins affecting others: "hatred, discord, jealousy, fits of rage, selfish ambition, dissensions, factions and envy."

When I was in the seventh grade, some of the other girls in my school hated me. They wrote bad things on the bathroom wall about me and did not invite me to participate in their parties. It bothered me for a while until I discovered the reason for their hatred—my boyfriend. The girls hated me because he liked me. You see, their hatred stemmed from jealously and led to discord, selfish ambition, and factions.

Simply stated, all of the above problems are contrary to the law of brotherly love. Unless handled immediately, personal feelings of hatred grow into the actions that are mentioned in the following list. Here are some of the signs that you may be succumbing to these sins:

- You can't help tossing a comment into the conversation that will start contention.
- You feel passionately indignant toward someone who really hasn't done anything wrong to you, and you lash out in anger whenever that person is around.
- You push yourself ahead with no regard to others around you.
- You have problems with the friendships others form without you.
- You are quick to pass on negative information you have heard about others.

Take yourself before God and go one by one down the list of these sins against your neighbor. Ask Him the hard question: Am I guilty of any of these?

## Sins Against Ourselves

The final section of the list discusses sins against ourselves: "drunkenness, orgies, and the like." These words suggest out-of-control, over-the-top behaviors that do not befit a child of God. Intoxication and wild behaviors are ungodly. Period. This doesn't mean you can't get together with your friends and have fun. But remember, you are first and foremost God's child. Even when you are out with your friends.

I love the way God has included other ideas of things you may be tempted to do by ending this list with the words "and the like."

Are you involved in activities that are sins against yourself? Ask God to reveal them to you. Confess them to God, and then clean up your act.

Remember where you came from. You were in bondage, and you didn't like it. Remember that you cried for God to deliver you, and He did. Nothing about bondage was sweet and comfortable, so nothing related to bondage should be allowed to come along with you into your promised land. Let go of the flesh willingly. And do it now!

By the way, I parted with the wedding gown. The antique satin probably brought a good price at a resale shop. My china replaced his, and I took pictures of the school projects so they'll be remembered for years to come.

# Nine

# Satisfaction

## What Should My Taste Buds Enjoy?

Now that you have unpacked your baggage and cleansed your palate of the leeks and onions, it's time to develop your taste for Promised Land food—a delicacy known as the fruit of the Spirit.

Galatians 5:22-23 explains that the fruit of the Spirit consists of "love, joy, peace, patience, kindness, goodness, faithfulness, gentleness and self-control." Notice that *fruit* is singular. The potential to possess all of these characteristics is yours once you surrender your life to God through Jesus Christ. Just as you were once capable of yielding to all the sins of the fleshly nature, you are now capable of replacing them with the fruit of the Spirit.

Since each element of the fruit is part of the whole, you will find that as you develop a taste for one element, another will begin to develop. For example, when you love the unlovable, you will find yourself exercising patience; when you bring kindness to bear upon a situation, you'll experience peace; and when you use self-control, you will become gentle.

I suppose you have noticed that I am not pushing you to *work* at developing the fruit of the Spirit. Just as fruit simply pops out of the kind of tree it is growing from, so the fruit of the Spirit will pop out of you because you are God's child. When properly watered, fertilized, and cared for, apples come from apple trees, lemons come from lemon trees, and oranges come from orange trees. When properly rooted and grounded in the Word of God, the fruit of the Spirit will come from your life too.

So how will you recognize the development of the fruit?

Love is from the Greek word *agape,* which means "affection or benevolence, charity, and dear love." This is God's kind of love—love that happens despite the circumstances. Exhibiting this kind of love without the power of the Holy Ghost is impossible. We are too judgmental, too self-centered, and too focused on our rights to offer agape love to anyone. Yet, living toward others with this kind of love is exactly what you will do when you allow the Spirit to control you.

You'll be surprised at how you will have a loving attitude toward the most cantankerous people. You'll shock others around you when you don't react negatively, although most other people would. When others express their indignation over certain situations, you sincerely won't feel that way. Agape love is in bloom.

**Start to journal about the incidents you notice when you react with agape love.**

*Joy* means "cheerfulness, calm delight, and gladness." If I had had a daughter, I would have named her Chara (pronounced Kah'rah), the Greek word for joy. God's joy exists in spite of circumstances. You'll know joy is maturing when you can smile when things don't turn out the way you planned and during trying times.

When my father died, my immediate family perplexed attendants at the funeral home while we were making his final arrangements. They figured our sudden tears were from grief, when actually one of their comments struck our funny bones. Ever try to suppress a laugh? Our eyes watered and cheeks reddened as we tried to retain our composure.

We could laugh because we had joy even though Daddy was gone. Yes, we missed him terribly, but we knew he was in heaven, healed and rejoicing. He was a happy man and would have laughed at the comment too. Even then, joy bubbled up in us.

Continue to journal. Add your unexpected joyful reactions when you are in stressful situations or when things don't turn out as you planned.

*Peace* means "quiet, rest, and to set at one again." This definition brings to my mind a pond that returns to stillness after the campers leave from swim practice.

The Bible never promises that you will be free of ripples in the pond, huge splashes, or even water displacement. But God does promise you that if you turn to Him, He will quiet the waves. In John 14:27 Jesus tells us, "Peace I leave with you; my peace I give you. I do not give to you as the world gives. Do not let your hearts be troubled and do not be afraid."

No matter what the circumstance, Jesus has given us peace, and it is up to us to allow that peace to quiet our hearts in troubled times. Think about it: When faced with vexing problems, we are unable to do anything about the situation anyway. Why not let the peace of the fruit of the Spirit carry us right then? You have nothing to lose and everything to gain.

Journal about times when you experience upheaval but God infuses peace you didn't expect.

*Long-suffering* or *patience* means "forbearance or fortitude." This is a tough one because you don't even need patience until something is wrong. You can tell positive stories about love, joy, and peace, but patience stories always include drama. You can love someone, experience a joyful day, and have a peaceful attitude when everything is going fine; but patience by definition means you are pushing through an issue.

I'm a chicken. I never pray for patience. Why? Because Rom. 5:3-4 says, "Knowing that tribulation worketh patience; and patience, experience; and experience, hope" (KJV). If I am praying for patience, I am asking for problems because that's the only way to see patience. It's sort of like testing glow-in-the-dark items. In order to see if they really work, you have to turn off all the lights. It's only in complete darkness that you can see if the thing glows.

Now you've read enough about my problems in this book to realize that just because I don't pray for patience doesn't mean I don't have problems. God loves me too much to let me sail through life without developing my character. I'm just trusting that the long-suffering element of the fruit of the Spirit is maturing as I mature in my walk with Him, and it will pop out when I need it.

Continue to journal. Write about times God helps you put up with things, forbear with people, and have patience through a difficult time.

*Gentleness/kindness* means "usefulness and moral excellence in character or demeanor." When I think of this element of the fruit of the Spirit, I think of the campaign that suggested that Americans be involved in doing random acts of kindness. This meant doing things not just because the action was deserved in some way but also just to be nice. Another way to say this is, "It's just nice to be nice."

I like to smile and make eye contact with people. I smile at others when I'm standing in the bank line, shopping in the mall, or sitting at a traffic light (and on Los Angeles highways, that's a pretty courageous thing to do). If the person smiles back, I'm likely to start a conversation and probably give a compliment. Those smiles and compliments seem to melt tension from the faces of the strangers I encounter. I like to think it is a result of the goodness of the fruit of the Spirit that pops out of my life onto others.

Another way to measure gentleness is by your words. Proverbs 15:1 says, "A gentle answer turns away wrath, but a harsh word stirs up anger." You will notice the maturation of gentleness when you do not shoot back harsh words at every opportunity. You no longer have to be the one to pull someone down to size with your cutting remark. The tongue is the toughest member of your body to tame. Study James 3:1-18 if you are having trouble with the words of your mouth. You will find that wisdom dictates a controlled tongue and gentle words come from a pure heart.

Write in your journal about the gentle things you catch yourself doing. Also write down gentle comments you make at times when you could think of something cutting or ugly to say.

*Goodness* means "virtue or beneficence." This is more an attribute of what you think than of what you do. This is who you are and good actions automatically proceed from you.

My husband spent a large part of his life in Kansas City. When we visited Kansas City with him for the first time, he took us to the Plaza, an upscale part of town that is full of designer boutiques. He told the boys they could each get one thing. They ended up selecting a few items of clothing.

As we talked about that excursion three years later, the boys said that, looking back, they were crazy to settle for such insignificant and inexpensive items. I told them they didn't even consider taking advantage of James's kindness because they were genuinely good boys who had not been raised to take advantage of the kindness of others.

You may not be able to journal about your own goodness because you won't even think of it as anything special. To you, you're just acting toward people the way you should. Unless it comes up in conversation—possibly years later, as in the example of our Plaza shopping trip—you may never know. Great. That's goodness at work.

*Faith/faithfulness* means "persuasion, assurance of the truth, belief, and fidelity." Faith is like an engagement ring. It represents what you cannot yet see—marriage—but there is the full assurance that it will take place. I had so much assurance when my husband proposed and gave me my beautiful ring that I began to plan the wedding, spending money on things I'd need for that day.

You'll recognize the faith element of the fruit of the Spirit when your faith in God moves you to act as if you already experience things that have not yet manifested themselves in reality.

Write in your journal about the things for which you are standing in faith. Leave a space to the right of each item to jot down the date God brings your faith to sight.

*Meekness/gentleness* means "mildness and humility." Meekness does not mean weakness. To the contrary, meekness is strength under control. For example, you could retaliate, but you choose to keep your cool. You are capable of cutting the teacher down to size who unjustly criticized your child, but you calmly steer the conversation to only the facts and reach an amicable understanding.

When you begin to see meekness in your life, you'll have begun conforming to the image of Christ. He was meek; His strength was always under control. Even while suffering the agony and indignity of the Cross, Jesus kept His cool. He could have called legions of angels to wipe out His murderers, but He chose to endure so that you and I could be saved. Hallelujah!

Journal about times when you see meekness at work in your life; times when you could have used your own verbal strength to handle things, but you felt the Holy Spirit helping you react in His strength instead.

The final element of the fruit of the Spirit is temperance or self-control. You need self-control to love unlovable folk, be gentle toward those who are harsh with you, and exercise patience when you want what you want right now. It also takes self-control to be good and to react meekly when you find yourself in situations where your flesh screams for you to let it take over. Self-control allows joy and peace to replace despair when your faith is challenged.

Look back at the last paragraph. Self-control is associated with all of the other eight elements of the fruit. I see self-control as the beautiful blossom that precedes the actual fruit itself. We don't need self-control simply for the sake of self-control. We need it when we are tempted to grab back the control of our lives from God so we can act any way we want to act. Self-control allows the fruit of the Spirit to operate instead of allowing human nature to get in the way.

When I was growing up, the older people at my church used to say, "The things I used to do, I don't do anymore." Your taste for the fruit of the Spirit—Promised Land food—will develop as the taste for leeks and onions decreases. Thank God. The transfer works.

# Ten
# Destination
## How Do I Consistently Live by This New Plan?

As Solomon said in Eccles. 12:13, "Let us hear the conclusion of the whole matter" (KJV). As you comfortably take your place in your new destination, free from whatever was holding you back, how do you guarantee that you will stay in this new place? Answer: Make a plan and follow it.

It always amazes me when I hear stories of people who suddenly come into lots of money and are broke six months later. Why didn't they sit down and draw up a strategy before they started to spend? Those people ended up in the same shape they were in before—maybe even worse shape.

You don't want the same thing to happen to you spiritually. You need a strategy. I've heard and so have you: If you fail to plan, you plan to fail. Now is not the time to become complacent; now's the time to get to work.

This new life has not been granted to you only for your enjoyment. God has saved you and moved you to this "location" in your life to do some good work for Him.

Consider Phil. 2:12-13, "Therefore . . . continue to work out your salvation with fear and trembling, for it is God who works in you to will and to act according to his good purpose." As Christ lives in you and as the Holy Spirit empowers you, you are responsible to live out what's on the inside.

I have found eight examples in Scripture of plans God gave His people to carry out for Him. I'm sure that's not all there are, but these give you a place to start as you explore what God has instilled in you and what He wants you to do with it.

# Raise Special Children

Mary and Joseph weren't expecting to be the parents of the Messiah. To be honest, most of us weren't fully ready for the specialness of each of our children either. But we've got the kids now, and God expects us to properly handle the incredible uniqueness of each one of them. If you have children, your calling is to focus on pointing them in the direction God has chosen for them. What specific things does God intend for you to do with the children He has given you?

# Go Somewhere

Abraham was told to leave his own country and his kindred and follow God into his future. God may be prompting you to make a move. This might be a physical move to a new house, city, state, or country. It could be a move to another job or relationship. Where is God telling you to go?

# Build Something

Noah was instructed to build an ark to the saving of his family. (See Gen. 6:14-18 and Heb. 11:7.) Perhaps God is telling you to build something. You might need to work on building a stronger marriage. Maybe you're to build habits into yourself or your children that will strengthen your faith. You may be led to build a ministry of some type. What might God be telling you to build?

# Accept Help

"The LORD God said, 'It is not good for the man to be alone. I will make a helper suitable for him'" (Gen. 2:18). The very first thing that was not good was singularity; Adam needed companionship and help. You may be the independent thinker with the motto, "I can do it all by myself," but that might not be what God wants. Immature two-year-olds are quick to spout that motto too. What assistance is God prompting you to accept?

## Say Something

In 1 Kings 3:16-27, Solomon judged shrewdly between two women to discern which one was the mother of the living child. God enabled him to operate wisely in his dealings with the people he ruled. All Solomon's sage wisdom would have had no effect, though, if he had kept his mouth shut. What is God moving upon you to say that will bring wisdom to a certain situation?

## Make a Choice

The prophet Samuel was in a tough spot. He had to find a king to rule God's people when the people should not even have wanted a king in the first place. (See 1 Sam. 8:1-9 for the background of this story.) You may be shying away from commitment because you refuse to buckle down and make a choice. You may be stagnating because you fear making a choice that will close the door on that which makes you comfortable. What choice is God moving you to make?

## Endure Something

Mary and Martha endured the grief of the death of their beloved brother Lazarus so that Jesus could show them something greater. (See John 11:1-45.) Psalm 30:5 encourages us by saying, "Weeping may endure for a night, but joy cometh in the morning" (KJV). Babies mature in the womb in the dark, and photographs reveal their images in the dark. God does some of His best work in our dark times, and what a blessing we receive when our spiritual mornings dawn. What is it that God is expecting you to endure?

## Conquer Something

Joshua was challenged to conquer Jericho. (See Josh. 6:1-5.) Maybe God is telling you it's time to conquer your addiction to cigarettes, alcohol, drugs, food, illicit sex, or whatever. It could be time to forgive; in other words, time to get over it. Perhaps there's a fear you need to conquer—fear of commitment, success, failure, or some such apprehension. What is there in your life that seems like an insurmountable obstacle? Is God telling you to conquer it?

Take these eight areas of planning to God in prayer. Perhaps one or more of them are areas God intends you to work on in your promised land. As He directs, make your plan by filling out the following chart.

|  | Things I plan to accomplish and places I plan to go | Things and places I plan to avoid | Preliminary plan to accomplish this. Goal or date to begin pursuing this goal |
|---|---|---|---|
| Within the next year |  |  |  |
| Within the next 5 years |  |  |  |
| Within the next 10 years |  |  |  |

Your new plan is in place. Rest in God, praise Jesus, and follow the leading of the Holy Spirit as you leave behind leeks and onions and live a milk-and-honey life.

# Notes

## Chapter 5

1. Gary Trent and John Smalley, *The Gift of the Blessing* (Nashville: Thomas Nelson, 1993), 18-19.

2. Charles Swindoll, *You and Your Child* (Nashville: Thomas Nelson, Bantam ed., 1980), 8-9.

3. Florence Littauer, *Raising Christians, Not Just Children* (Dallas: Word Publishing, 1988).

## Chapter 6

1. Oswald Chambers, *My Utmost for His Highest* (Barbour Publishing, Inc., 1935, 1963).

## Chapter 7

1. From *Matthew Henry's Commentary on the Whole Bible,* online edition, comments related to John 1:4.

## Chapter 8

1. From *Matthew Henry's Commentary,* comments related to Gal. 5:19.